PHIGS by Example

W.A. Gaman   W.A. Giovinazzo

PHIGS by Example

With 26 Figures

Springer-Verlag
New York Berlin Heidelberg London
Paris Tokyo Hong Kong Barcelona

William A. Gaman
Alliant Computer Systems
 Corporation
67 Los Trancos Road
Portola Valley, CA 94028
USA

William A. Giovinazzo
Simplified Optical Systems
225 West Torrence Boulevard
Carson, CA 90745
USA

The cover art was generated by the authors on an Alliant GX4000 based on a Sun 4/260 using the PHIGS/PHIGS+ examples contained within this book.

Printed on acid-free paper.

Camera-ready copy prepared using Microsoft Word 4.0 for the Macintosh and MacDraw.
Printed and bound by R.R. Donnelley & Sons, Harrisonburg, VA.
Printed in the United States of America.

9 8 7 6 5 4 3 2 1

ISBN 0-387-97555-1 Springer-Verlag New York Berlin Heidelberg
ISBN 3-540-97555-1 Springer-Verlag Berlin Heidelberg New York

To Our Families for Putting Up with Us
Ryan, Shayna, Teresa, John
Carol, Diana

Contents

Introduction

The Programmer's Hierarchical Interactive Graphics System (PHIGS) is a computer-graphics standard defining an interface between an application program and a computer-graphics system. PHIGS has been actively under development since 1980. Much of this development has been performed by Technical Committee X3H3 under the American National Standard Institute (ANSI) procedures. PHIGS is also an international standard sponsored by the United States and developed by the international computer-graphics committee, ISO TC97/SC21/WG2. In addition, PHIGS has been selected as the graphics extension to the X-window standard and as part of the Intel i860 P.A.X. standard.

The PHIGS standard has received wide acceptance throughout the computer-graphics industry. PHIGS libraries are available on most of the high-performance three-dimensional graphics platforms. These include IBM, DEC, HP, Sun, Alliant, Stardent, and Silicon Graphics. Despite this acceptance, there are few texts that provide the software engineer with an overview of the standard. The only currently available PHIGS references are in the form of the ANSI functional description, technical papers, and device-specific PHIGS documentation. These are of little help to the novice PHIGS programmer.

Reference manuals are terrific for the function for which they are designed, a listing of detailed information concerning specific functions. These references are lacking, however, as a source for understanding the overall standard. It is one thing to know all of the parts in a plane; it is quite another to know how those parts are put together to create an aircraft. A reference manual describes the parts; *PHIGS by Example* tells you how to make it fly!

PHIGS by Example is designed to meet the needs of the software engineer who is a novice in programming with PHIGS. The book does not present the reader with basic graphics programming concepts. *Fundamentals of Interactive Computer Graphics*, by Foley and Van Dam, or *Principals of Interactive Computer Graphics,* by Newman and Sproull, have long been established as the best general computer-graphics texts. *PHIGS by Example* teaches the application programmer how to use the PHIGS standard in his or her own program.

We have based the structure and content of *PHIGS by Example* on years of struggling with PHIGS and teaching PHIGS to others. This experience has shown that the best way to learn PHIGS is to use PHIGS. We have, therefore, built each section around programming examples. Each section begins with a conceptual discussion of the PHIGS topic presented in that section. This is followed by a detailed explanation of an example program or subroutine. The chapters are concluded with a set of exercises that will challenge the reader to experiment with the PHIGS function described in that section. We strongly urge the reader to experiment with each of these examples beyond the recommended exercises.

It is important to emphasize the benefits of the examples presented in each section. Examples show the reader how the PHIGS functions are invoked, as well as the interaction between each of the functions. Examples also demonstrate, in a very clear and precise manner, the procedures necessary to create PHIGS effects, such as rotation, color approximation, etc. The most important benefit, however, is that the readers are left with a "tool kit" of graphics utility subroutines that they may call from their programs.

In several locations in the text, we have inserted the phrase *"STOP AND THINK ABOUT THIS."* This comment is to direct the reader to PHIGS concepts that require special consideration. Having read our own share of technical documents, we are aware that certain key concepts can be glossed over.

For the sake of clarity, we have also avoided the more cryptic features of the C language, such as `i+=1`. While many readers may be proficient in C, we have kept the examples as simple as possible to avoid any confusion and to facilitate its translation to FORTRAN.

WAG I
WAG II

1
Drawing with PHIGS

Introduction

This chapter provides the reader with some basic concepts in PHIGS. On completion of this chapter the reader will be able to create a graphic object and change its appearance.

The Programmer's Hierarchical Interactive Graphics System (PHIGS) is a computer-graphics standard defining an interface between an application program and a computer-graphics system. As can be seen in Figure 1.1, the application program interacts with PHIGS by making PHIGS function calls. PHIGS, in turn, interacts with the underlying graphics system. This frees the application programmer from concern over the individual details of the graphics subsystem. Graphics programming with PHIGS deals with a set of objects (structures, structure elements, and workstations) and operations on those objects (transforming, posting, editing, and closing). The programmer can now think in object-oriented[1] terms.

In order to access any of the PHIGS functions, the software engineer must first "open" PHIGS and a workstation. When finished, PHIGS and the workstation must be closed. The open and closed combinations create different PHIGS states. Section 1.1 describes each of these concepts.

Graphic objects are created and manipulated in *structure*. Just as PHIGS and workstations are opened and closed, so are structures. A structure may contain different types of *structure elements*, which are the smallest unit of graphic information. These structure elements are stored in display list memory (DLM). The first of these structure elements are output primitives. There are seven types of output primitives. Section 1.2 will demonstrate how to create the most basic structure.

---

[1]Nielsen, K. and Shumate, K: *Designing Large Real-Time Systems with Ada,* McGraw-Hill, New York, 1988. Also, see Booch, G.: Object-oriented development, IEEE Transactions on Software Engineering, vol. SE 12, no. 2, February 1986.

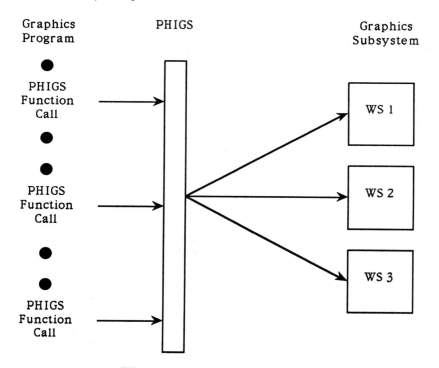

Figure 1.1. PHIGS interface.

Before an object is drawn on a workstation, a structure that is stored in DLM must be *posted_* to a workstation. Posting a structure to a workstation identifies on which workstation the structure is to be displayed. Objects are drawn on a workstation by up dating the workstation. When a workstation is updated, objects posted to it will be drawn on its display surface. The process of posting a structure and updating the workstation is described in Section 1.3.

*Attributes_* are structure elements that define the appearance of an object. Each output primitive is associated with a set of attributes. Section 1.4 will demonstrate the use of these attributes and their effects on the output primitives with which they are associated.

Examples are presented at the end of each section. The PHIGS function calls that are discussed in each section are printed in boldface type in each of the examples. The first two examples will not create an image on the screen, these examples are presented to familiarize the reader with PHIGS states.

Table 1.1. PHIGS state table.

State	PHIGS	Workstation	Structure	Archive
PHCL,WSCL,STCL,ARCL	Closed	Closed	Closed	Closed
PHOP,WSCL,STCL,ARCL	Open	Closed	Closed	Closed
PHOP,WSOP,STCL,ARCL	Open	Open	Closed	Closed
PHOP,WSOP,STOP,ARCL	Open	Open	Open	Closed
PHOP,WSOP,STOP,AROP	Open	Open	Open	Open
PHOP,WSOP,STCL,AROP	Open	Open	Closed	Open
PHOP,WSCL,STOP,AROP	Open	Closed	Open	Open
PHOP,WSCL,STOP,ARCL	Open	Closed	Open	Closed
PHOP,WSCL,STCL,AROP	Open	Closed	Closed	Open

1.1 Getting Started with PHIGS

PHIGS is a computer-graphics standard that defines the interface between a computer-graphics program and a computer-graphics system. PHIGS can be described as a *finite state machine.*[2] A finite state machine is a system with a specific number of states and state changes. Within PHIGS, there are four states: PHIGS; workstation; structure; and archive. The combination of these four states creates an overall PHIGS state in which the program executes. The different PHIGS modes are listed in Table 1.1. A state is entered by being opened and exited by being closed.

As the different PHIGS functions are presented throughout this text, the required states will be specified. We will use PHOP, WSOP, STOP, and AROP to represent PHIGS open, workstation open, structure open, and archive open, respectively. Similarly, the closed states are presented as PHCL, WSCL, STCL, and ARCL. The components of the PHIGS states will always be presented in this order. An asterisk will signify that the state of this component is not significant to the PHIGS function, essentially a "Don't Care."

As shown in Figure 1.2, all states are a subset of, or subordinate to, PHIGS OPEN. Therefore, in order to perform any operations in PHIGS, including the opening of the other states, you need to be in the PHIGS open state, PHOP. Within each of the subordinate states, we are also able to open any of the other states. For example, from the PHIGS open and workstation open states, we can open a structure, archive, or another workstation. As seen in Table 1.1, this creates the possibility of nine different PHIGS states. To understand the practical application of these concepts, let's look at Programming Example 1.1.

---

[2]Nielsen, K. and Shumate, K: *Designing Large Real-Time Systems with Ada,* McGraw-Hill, New York, 1988.

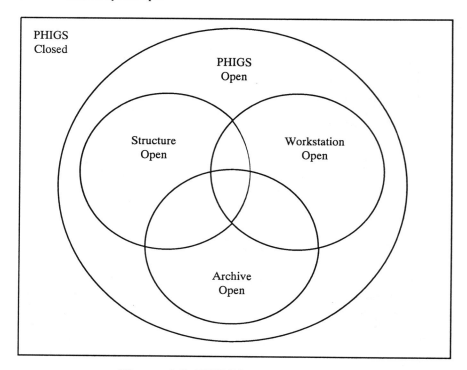

Figure 1.2. PHIGS state diagram.

Programming Example 1.1

Programming Example 1.1 is a very simple PHIGS program that demonstrates the PHIGS states as well as the order in which these states must be opened and closed. The program opens and closes a PHIGS workstation. According to the PHIGS state rules, PHIGS must be open in order to open a workstation. The workstation must be closed prior to closing PHIGS.

The program begins with the inclusion of the PHIGS library:

#include <phigs.h>

This is an enumeration file that contains the PHIGS data structures and constants that are called by the application program.

Opening PHIGS

The example program opens PHIGS and initializes the PHIGS environment with the following function call:

popenphigs ("/dev/tty", 0);

Prior to issuing this call, PHIGS must be closed (PHCL, WSCL, STCL, ARCL). The initialization of the PHIGS environment sets the system state to PHIGS open, (PHOP, WSCL, STCL, ARCL). Entering the PHIGS open state allocates and initializes the *PHIGS State List*. The popenphigs function also makes the *PHIGS Description Table* and the *Workstation Description Table* available. The contents of each of these tables are presented in Table 1.2. Although detailed knowledge about these tables is not necessary at this point, the information is presented here for completeness.

The first parameter to the popenphigs call, "/dev/tty", is the filename of the file that receives PHIGS error messages. This parameter is a character string or a pointer to a character string that specifies the name of the error file. The file /dev/tty defaults to the current output device in UNIX®, other operating systems may require a different pathname. The filename is stored in the PHIGS Error State List. Check the value required for this parameter by your PHIGS implementation.

Table 1.2. PHIGS control tables.

PHIGS state list

List of open workstations
List of open archive files
Name of open structure
Element pointer
Current structure edit mode
Input queue device

PHIGS description table

Systems resource list
List of available workstations & types
List of available character sets
List of GSEs
System resource limits listed
Inquire to read available system resources
Set of default PHIGS states

Workstation description table

Set of default workstation states
Workstation dependent resource limits
INQUIRE to read available workstation resources

®UNIX is a registered trademark of AT&T Bell Laboratories in the United States and other countries.

The second parameter, 0, specifies the amount of memory units for a buffer area. In the example, the system's PHIGS library automatically allocates the memory needed. Check the value required for this parameter by your PHIGS implementation.

Opening a WORKSTATION

Now that PHIGS is open, the program may open a workstation, structure, or archive. In Programming Example 1.1, the program opens a workstation with the following function call:

popenws (WS_ID, 0, PWST_OUTPUT_TRUE);

Execution of this function opens a workstation, which is identified by WS_ID of the type PWST_OUTPUT_TRUE. This places PHIGS in the workstation open state, (PHOP, WSOP, STCL, ARCL). In this state, the program can open another workstation, a structure or an archive.

Before we discuss what this function does, we must first understand what is meant by a workstation. A PHIGS workstation is an abstraction of some graphical resource. It is through this graphics resource that the application program interfaces with the actual physical device. In short, do not think of a workstation as a physical device (keyboard, terminal, and remote system), but as an abstraction of some resource to be used by your program. This resource can be anything from a window on your screen where objects are drawn to a digitizing table from which data are read. It is merely some entity with which your program is going to work. In the example program the workstation that is opened is an output window on the screen of our graphics device. Two or more workstations (i.e., output windows) may be opened simultaneously on the same graphics device.

When this call is executed, PHIGS creates a workstation with the identifier specified by the parameter WS_ID. Note that this is an input value. In our example, we have used the identifier 1 to identify the workstation we are opening. When we refer to workstation 1 while we are in this state, we are referring to the workstation we have just opened.

The second parameter is the connection identifier. In a multiscreen configuration[3] the connection identifier indicates on which screen the workstation is to be opened, PHIGS accepts two values for the connection identifier, either **NULL** (0) or Pconnid. The Pconnid data type is a structure, which is defined in phigs.h as follows:

```
typedef struct {
        int conn_type;
     union {
        int screen;
```

---

[3]A multiscreen configuration is the use of more than one physical terminal by a single application.

```
    } connection
} *Pconnid;
```

Since these examples are written for a single screen environment the **NULL** value (0) is used in this call for the connection identifier parameter.

The third parameter of the popenws function is the workstation type, which specifies the type of workstation that is to be opened. There are three characteristics specified by this parameter: (1) type of input/output; (2) type of color; and (3) type of buffering supported by the workstation. The eight different combinations of these values accepted by PHIGS are presented in Table 1.3. In the example, we have used the value PWST_OUTPUT_TRUE. This value specifies an output-only workstation which is true-color and single-buffered. The workstation types are defined in the phigs.h include file.

In creating the workstation PHIGS allocates and initializes the *Workstation State List*. The data within this list can be modified by the application program. The *Workstation State Variable* describes the current state of the workstation. Since it is stored in the workstation state list, and the state list exists only for a workstation which is opened, the Workstation State Variable is always set to open, or WSOP.

In addition to the Workstation State List which is described above, the popenws PHIGS function also creates a *Workstation Description Table*. The workstation description table (Table 1.2) includes the workstation type parameter as well as information obtained from the device and implementation-dependent information. The data contained in the Workstation Description Table

Table 1.3. Workstation types.

Workstation type	Characteristics
PWST_OUTPUT_PSEUDO	Output-only, pseudo-color,single buffered
PWST_OUTPUT_PSEUDO_DB	Output-only, pseudo-color, double-buffered
PWST_OUTPUT_TRUE	Output-only, true-color, single-buffered
PWST_OUTPUT_TRUE_DB	Output-only, true-color, double-buffered
PWST_OUTIN_PSEUDO	Output and input, pseudo-color, single-buffered
PWST_OUTIN_PSEUDO_DB	Output and input, pseudo-color, Double-buffered
PWST_OUTIN_TRUE	Output and input, true-color, single-buffered
PWST_OUTIN_TRUE_DB	Output and input, true-color, Double-buffered

describe the capabilities of the workstation being opened. The specific structure the workstation description table is not as important at this point as is the knowledge that it exist.

Once the workstation state list and the workstation description table have been created, PHIGS adds the workstation identifier to the list of open workstations in the PHIGS state list. PHIGS then opens the workstation on the device that is identified by the connection identifier. The newly created workstation has the characteristics defined by the workstation description table.

PHIGS does not allow us to have direct access to the workstation description table or any of the state lists. We can, however, examine the data contained in these structures through *Inquire* functions. These functions read the values contained in the state lists and description tables. Inquire functions are useful in determining the state, characteristics, and capabilities of the graphics system, as well as in determining error conditions.

Closing a Workstation

Now that the sample program has opened PHIGS and a workstation, the program can continue to perform any variety of PHIGS functions. In the interest of simplicity the example closes the workstation with the following function call:

pclosews (WS_ID);

The pclosews function requires that PHIGS and the workstation identified by WS_ID both be open (PHOP, WSOP, *, *).

When a workstation is closed, all associated references to the workstation elsewhere in PHIGS are removed. The workstation is implicitly updated with all actions that have been deferred; this is discussed in more detail in Section 1.3. The workstation state list is deallocated and the workstation identifier is removed from the list of open workstations.

If the workstation is of type OUTIN, the input queue is flushed of all events from all devices associated with the workstation. The Workstation Description Table becomes unavailable and the workstation-type value associated with this workstation description table becomes undefined. Closing the workstation finishes when the connection to the workstation is released. The state of the example program at this point is PHIGS open (PHOP, WSCL, STCL, ARCL).

Closing PHIGS

The PHIGS state is closed with the following PHIGS function call:

pclosephigs ();

This function sets the PHIGS state to closed, (PHCL, WSCL, STCL, ARCL). To execute this function call, all workstations, structures, and archives must be closed. When PHIGS is closed the PHIGS description table, the PHIGS state list, and the workstation description table become unavailable. All PHIGS buffers are released and all PHIGS files are closed.

```
/*
 *                      Example 1.1⁴
 */
#include <phigs.h>

#define      WS_ID        1       /*PHIGS Workstation ID Number */

main()
{
   /* Open PHIGS
    * System will be in state (PHOP,WSCL,STCL,ARCL) */
   popenphigs ("/dev/tty", 0);

   /* Open a true-color workstation
    * System will be in state (PHOP,WSOP,STCL,ARCL) */
   popenws (WS_ID, 0, PWST_OUTPUT_TRUE);

   /* Close the workstation
    * System will be in state (PHOP,WSCL,STCL,ARCL) */
   pclosews (WS_ID);

   /* Close PHIGS
    * System will be in state (PHCL,WSCL,STCL,ARCL) */
   pclosephigs ();
}
```

1.2 Creating a Structure

Graphic objects are created and manipulated in *structures*. A structure is a sequence of *structure elements* that describe a graphic object. The following is a list of the different types of structure elements:

>Output primitives
>Attributes
>Labels

---

[4]In order to be consistent with PHIGS, the British spelling of color, *colour,* has been preserved in the programming examples.

Application data
Name set specifications
Transformation selections
View selections
Structure invocations

When we create a graphic object, we build a structure. The building blocks of the structure are structure elements that define different characteristics of the graphic object. Some of these characteristics are the shape, color, and orientation of the graphic object. Once the structure has been opened, all subsequent structure elements are stored in the *Centralized Structure Store* (CSS) in sequential order until the structure is closed.

In Figure 1.3 we show graphically how a typical PHIGS structure is created. The pseudo code first opens a structure. It then makes PHIGS function calls to define the attributes of the output primitive. The example in the figure defines the color, linewidth, and line-type attributes of the output primitive. After all the attributes have been defined, the program generates an output primitive. We will look at this process more closely in the example.

The first structure element with which we will work is the *output primitive*. An output primitive consist of those PHIGS functions that are used to construct an object. There are seven types of output primitives, they are:

Polyline
Polymarker
Text
Annotation Text
Fill Area
Fill Area Set
Cell Array

Refer to Table 1.4 for a definition of each of these examples.

The examples we present in this chapter use the polyline output primitive. The polyline output primitive defines a set of connected lines whose position is defined by the coordinates of the endpoints of the lines. Now that we understand structures and structure elements, we are ready to see how they are used in a program. Let's now look at Programming Example 1.2.

Programming Example 1.2

Programming Example 1.2 first opens PHIGS and a workstation. The program then opens a structure and calls the user subroutine create_polyline. When control returns to the calling program, the structure, workstation, and PHIGS are closed. Although the example closes the structure before the workstation, it is not necessary that it be done in this order. Both the workstation and the structure, however, need to be closed prior to closing PHIGS.

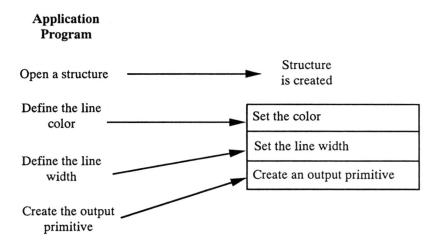

Application Program

Open a structure ⟶ Structure is created

Define the line color ⟶ Set the color

Set the line width

Define the line width ⟶ Create an output primitive

Create the output primitive

Figure 1.3. Structure creation.

Open a PHIGS Structure

Prior to calling the subroutine create_polyline, the program opens a structure with the following function call:

```
popenstruct (STRUCT_ID);
```

This function call requires that PHIGS is open and all structures are closed (PHOP, *, STCL, *).[5] Since the required PHIGS state is structure, closed, only one structure may be open at a time.

The popenstruct function receives, as input, the structure ID, STRUCT_ID. When the function is executed, PHIGS checks to see if the structure is a new structure which is being created or if it is an already existing structure that is being reopened for editing. In the example, the structure is being opened for the first time, so it is created. We will discuss structure-editing in Chapter 3.

PHIGS stores structures in a CSS. The CSS can be thought of as a database of structures that can be displayed on any open workstation. Structures in the CSS can also be opened for editing. The CSS is a storage area that is independent of all workstations and contains all structures and structure networks that have previously been created. Structure networks are covered in detail in Chapter 3.

When a structure is opened, it is associated with an element pointer. The element pointer points to the last element in the structure, if the structure being

---

[5]An asterisk in the state description indicates that it does not matter if the component is opened or closed.

Table 1.4. PHIGS output primitive.

Polyline	A set of connected lines defined by a series of endpoints	
Polymarker	Symbols centered at given positions	
	○ • * + X	
Text	A character string at a given position	PHIGS BY EXAMPLE
Fill area	A single, polygonal area, filled in a variety of styles, with or without edges	
Fill area set	A set of fill area that may be filled with differing interior styles, with or without edges	
Cell array	A parallelogram of equal sized cells, each of which is a parallelogram with a single color	
Annotation text	A character string at a given X-Y position where the characters are always parallel to the view X-Y plane	PHIGS BY EXAMPLE

opened already exists. The element pointer is useful when editing a structure. Newly created structures are empty structures, that is, the structure contains no structure elements. The element pointer, therefore, points to element 0.

Creating a Polyline Output Primitive

In this section we create our first structure element, which is a polyline output primitive. The following function call creates a polyline:

```
ppolyline (2, pts);
```

PHIGS requires that both PHIGS and a structure be opened (PHOP, *, STOP, *).

The first input received by the function is the numbers of points used to create the polyline. The second input is a list of vertices (coordinates of the line endpoints) passed to ppolyline in a structure array of points. The structure Ppoint is defined in phigs.h as:

```
typedef struct {
        Pfloat x;
        Pfloat y;
} Ppoint;
```

As can be seen by the above structure, points are expressed in terms of X and Y coordinates. Since this is a two-dimensional (2-D) polyline, there is no Z coordinate specified. When working in two dimensions PHIGS assumes Z to be 0. Prior to making the ppolyline function call, we load the structure array with the coordinates for points (0.25, 0.50) and (0.75, 0.50). This will create a line parallel to the X axis at 0.5Y which extends from 0.25X to 0.75X. We will see in Chapter 2 how these coordinates are transformed to represent screen coordinates.

Now that we have created a structure element, structure 1 is no longer empty. At this point we can continue to create structure elements, modify the structure, or close the structure. Since we are presenting a simple step by step approach to PHIGS, we will be satisfied with closing the structure.

Closing a Structure

After the structure element has been created, control returns to the main program. The program closes the structure with the following PHIGS function call:

```
pclosews (WS_ID);
```

The function receives no input parameters. Remember that PHIGS allows us to open only one structure at a time. The pclosestruct function closes the structure that is currently open. In order to make this function call, PHIGS and a structure must be open (PHOP, *, STOP, *). Once this function has been executed, the PHIGS state will change to structure closed (PHOP, *, STCL, *).

After the structure has been closed, control of the example program returns to the main program. In the main program, the workstation and PHIGS are closed, as is described in Section 1.1.

```
/*
 *                 Example 1.2
 */
#include <phigs.h>

#define      WS_ID       1        /* PHIGS Workstation ID Number */
#define      STRUCT_ID   1        /* PHIGS Structure ID Number   */

main()
{
    /* Open PHIGS
     * System will be in state (PHOP,WSCL,STCL,ARCL) */
    popenphigs ("/dev/tty", 0);

    /* Open a true-color workstation
     * System will be in state (PHOP,WSOP,STCL,ARCL) */
    popenws (WS_ID, 0, PWST_OUTPUT_TRUE);

    /* Open a structure to contain the output primitive.
     * System will be in state (PHOP,WSOP,STOP,ARCL) */
    popenstruct (STRUCT_ID);

    /* Draw the polyline */
    create_polyline ();

    /* Close the structure containing the polyline primitive.
     * System will be in state (PHOP,WSOP,STCL,ARCL) */
    pclosestruct ();

    /* Close the workstation
     * System will be in state (PHOP,WSCL,STCL,ARCL) */
    pclosews (WS_ID);

    /* Close PHIGS
     * System will be in state (PHCL,WSCL,STCL,ARCL) */
    pclosephigs ();
}
```

```
create_polyline ()
{
#include <phigs.h>

    Ppoint vertex[2]; /* Ppoint is a C structure defined
                       * in phigs.h */

    /* Initialize polyline position  Use X and
     * Y coordinates of end points. These endpoints are
     * called polyline vertices */
    vertex[0].x = 0.25;
    vertex[0].y = 0.50;
    vertex[1].x = 0.75;
    vertex[1].y = 0.50;

    /* Output the polyline primitive containing the
     * endpoints */
    ppolyline (2, vertex);
}
```

1.3 Drawing

If you execute Programming Example 1.2, you may notice that nothing becomes visible on the screen. In order to create an image on the display surface, we must first identify on which workstation the structure is to be drawn. We do this by *posting* a structure which is stored in the CSS. Posting identifies on which workstation a structure or structure network is to be drawn. This is shown graphically in Figure 1.4. A structure that has been posted does not become visible until the workstation to which it has been posted is updated. A structure is made visible at a workstation when the application program issues the redraw all structures or update workstation function call.

Programming Example 1.3

In Programming Example 1.3, we have changed the main program to post and update the newly created structure. After the structure is closed, it is posted to the workstation. The program then updates the workstation. This causes the structure to be shown on the display surface.

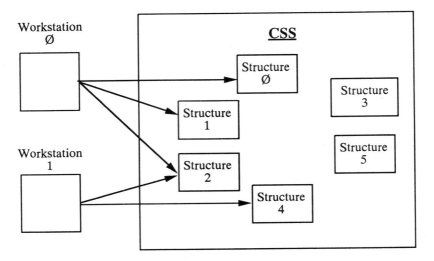

Figure 1.4. Centralized structure store.

Posting a Structure to a Workstation

Posting a structure requires PHIGS and the workstation to which the structure is posted to be open (PHOP, WSOP, *, *). The subroutine begins by posting the structure to the workstation with the following PHIGS function call:

ppoststruct (WS_ID, STRUCT_ID, priority);

The ppoststruct function posts the structure identified by STRUCT_ID and any associated structure network to the workstation. PHIGS performs this assignment by adding the structure ID to the *Table of Posted Structures* in the workstation state list. If the structure that is identified by STRUCT_ID does not exist, PHIGS will create an empty structure for that ID and post it.

The priority of the structure, specified by the third parameter to the function call, determines the importance of displaying the structure in relation to other structures that have been posted to the workstation. Structures of higher priority preempt the displaying of structures with a lower priority, the highest priority structure is drawn last so that it will not be covered by a lower priority structure. The lower the value of the priority variable the higher the priority of the posted structure. If two structures are posted with the same priority, the structure that was posted last is given the higher priority. Note that the priority scheme is different than the hidden-line/hidden-surface removal used in the modeling of solid objects. Hidden lines and surfaces are discussed in Chapter 4.

Once a structure is posted to a workstation, it remains posted to that workstation until the workstation is closed, the structure is specifically unposted, or the structure is deleted from the CSS. If a posted structure is opened for editing, the structure will remain posted.

Drawing the Structure on the Workstation

We are now ready to draw the structure. The program uses the following PHIGS function call to draw all the structures that have been posted to the workstation (WS_ID):

```
predrawallstruct (WS_ID, PALWAYS);
```

PHIGS requires that both PHIGS and a workstation be opened (PHOP, WSOP, *, *).

The second parameter to the function is a control flag to tell PHIGS whether the display surface is to be automatically cleared before redrawing the structure. This is an enumeration data type defined in phigs.h[6] as having the values PCONDITIONALLY or PALWAYS. When the value passed to predrawallstruct is set to PALWAYS, as in the example, the display surface is always cleared before the posted structures are drawn. If the value is set to PCONDITIONALY, the display surface is cleared only if it is not empty. This is useful in avoiding unnecessarily clearing an empty display surface. Generally, PALWAYS is used for CRTs and PCONDITIONALLY is used for plotters, where the time to clear the surface can be significant.

When we initiate the drawing of all structures to a workstation, PHIGS *traverses* the structures that have been posted to that workstation. The traversal process sequentially interprets each structure element, starting with the first. During the traversal process, the structure elements are interpreted for the workstation to which the structure has been posted. This means that the data contained in the structure elements, such as a color attribute or a transformation, are applied in relation to the workstation's attributes, such as the workstation's color approximation table or the workstation transformation, respectively. These concepts will become clearer as we become more familiar with workstation attributes and their effect on structure traversal. After the structure has been posted control returns to the main program. The main program then closes the workstation and PHIGS prior to termination.

Updating a Workstation

Updating a workstation also displays structures on a workstation. Although it is not used in the example, we have included it here for completeness. Both PHIGS and the workstation must be open (PHOP, WSOP, *, *) to update a workstation. The program performs the operation with the following function call:

```
pupdatews (WS_ID, PPERFORM);
```

---

[6]Note that the names declared in phigs.h begin with a "P" and are in upper case. It is best to avoid using these for user variable names.

The pupdate function updates the workstation that is identified by the workstation ID, WS_ID. Updating a workstation performs all actions that have been described for that workstation since the workstation was opened or since it was last updated.

```
/*
 *              Example 1.3
 */
#include <phigs.h>

#define      WS_ID       1      /* PHIGS Workstation ID Number */
#define      STRUCT_ID   1      /* PHIGS Structure ID Number   */

main()
{
  static int   priority = 0.0;
                    /* Structure display priority */

    /* Open PHIGS
     * System will be in state (PHOP,WSCL,STCL,ARCL) */
    popenphigs ("/dev/tty", 0);

    /* Open a true-color workstation
     * System will be in state (PHOP,WSOP,STCL,ARCL) */
    popenws (WS_ID, 0, PWST_OUTPUT_TRUE);

    /* Open a structure to contain the output primitive.
     * System will be in state (PHOP,WSOP,STOP,ARCL) */
    popenstruct (STRUCT_ID);

    /* Draw the polyline */
    create_polyline ();

    /* Close the structure containing the polyline primitive.
     * System will be in state (PHOP,WSOP,STCL,ARCL) */
    pclosestruct ();

    /* Post the structure to the open workstation */
    ppoststruct (WS_ID, STRUCT_ID, priority);
```

```
/* Redraw all structures posted to the workstation -
 * This is the command that begins traversal of the
 * structure network (in this case a single structure) */
predrawallstruct (WS_ID, PALWAYS);

/* Sleep a while to let operator see the display */
sleep (5);

/* Close the workstation
 * System will be in state (PHOP,WSCL,STCL,ARCL) */
pclosews (WS_ID);

/* Close PHIGS
 * System will be in state (PHCL,WSCL,STCL,ARCL) */
pclosephigs ();
}
```

1.4 Structure Attribute

So far, we have learned how to open a workstation and draw a structure on that workstation. We have also learned that output primitives are structure elements used to create graphic objects. *Attributes* are a type of structure element that control the appearance of output primitives. Output primitives are bound to the attributes when they are created during structure traversal. There are four types of attributes: *geometric*; *nongeometric, viewing,* and *identification.*

Geometric attributes control the shape or size of output primitives. An example of a geometric attribute is those attributes that control the height of characters for a text output primitive. The output primitive is the text, and the character height is the attribute. These attributes are independent of the workstation to which the structure is posted.

Nongeometric attributes control the appearance aspects of the output primitive. These attributes often deal with the color or the characteristics of the component parts of the output primitive. When specifying nongeometric aspects of an output primitive, the application program may set the *aspect source flag* (ASF) to indicate whether the attribute selection is selected from either an *attribute bundle*, or as an individual attribute selection.

The initial value of the ASF is dependent on the PHIGS implementation. If the program sets the ASF to individual, the value used for the attribute is that which is specified by the attribute structure element. If the program sets the ASF to bundled, the value used is the value that is specified in a bundle of attributes that it indicated by the bundle index. In the following examples, it has been assumed that the ASF has been set to individual. We will discuss setting the ASF in Chapter 4.

Viewing attributes are used in relation to workstation operations. Identification attributes are used for picking primitives with an input device. Although both of these attributes are important, we are not ready to discuss their significance at this point.

Programming Example 1.4

In Programming Example 1.4 we use the same object that we created in the previous examples and draw it to the same workstation. The only difference in Programming Example 1.4 is the specification of polyline attributes. The main program and other subroutines called by the main program are the same as in the previous examples.

The program has been modified to call the subroutine create_polyline_attributes. The create_polyline_attributes subroutine creates three structure elements that define the color, width, and line-type attributes for the polyline output primitive. The output primitive has no geometric attributes. The only nongeometric attributes for a polyline are color, width, and type.

Color Attribute

The color attribute is set by the following function call:

psetlinecolourind (colour_index);

Both PHIGS and the structure must be open (PHOP, *, STOP *) in order to make this function call.

The function receives, as input, an integer value that is an index to the defined color representation on the workstation state list. The color representation values are initialized from the workstation description table when the workstation is opened. The color value defined by the index will be applied to the output primitive when the ASF is set to individual. If the ASF is set to bundled, the color for the polyline will be taken from the bundle.

Line Type Attributes

After the color of the line has been set, the subroutine specifies the line type that is to be created with the following function call:

psetlinetype (line_type);

PHIGS requires both PHIGS and a structure be open (PHOP, *, STOP, *) to make this function call. The line type defined by this function will be applied to the output primitive when the ASF flag is set to individual. If the ASF is set to bundled, the line type will be taken from the bundle. The function receives, as input, an integer value that specifies the line type. The example has specified a line type of one, which is a solid line. Table 1.5 describes the line types.

Table 1.5. Line types.

Type	Description	Line
1	Solid	————
2	Dashed	— — —
3	Dotted	··········
4	Dash-Dotted	·—·—·—·—·

Line Width Attribute

The final attribute to be set for the polyline output primitive is the linewidth. When setting the width of the line, we do not specify the actual width in pixels.[7] PHIGS specifies lines in terms of a scaling factor that is applied to the nominal linewidth as defined in the workstation description table. Remember that the description table knows the capabilities of the workstation and should know better than the application program what is the optimal width of the line. The application program specifies only in relation to that optimal width. The following function call specifies this scaling factor:

```
psetlinewidth (width);
```

As with the first two attributes, PHIGS requires that PHIGS and a structure be opened (PHOP, *, STOP, *).

In the following example, the default linewidth for the workstation is one pixel. With a scale factor of 2, the width of the polyline to be drawn is two pixels. As we have seen with the two previous attributes, this attribute is applied only if the ASF is set to individual. If the ASF is set to bundle, the scale factor for linewidth is defined by the bundle.

After the linewidth has been set, control returns to the calling program. The rest of the program has remained unchanged, so execution continues as it had in the previous example. The polyline output primitive is created and posted to a workstation where it is drawn. The program then terminates after closing PHIGS and the workstation.

---

[7]The image frame is stored as a rectangular array of picture elements. A pixel is an individual picture element.

```
/*
 *                  Example 1.4
 */
#include <phigs.h>

#define      WS_ID         1      /* PHIGS Workstation ID Number */
#define      STRUCT_ID     1      /* PHIGS Structure ID Number   */

main()
{
    static int    priority = 0.0;
                                        /* Structure display priority */

    /* Open PHIGS
     * System will be in state (PHOP,WSCL,STCL,ARCL) */
    popenphigs ("/dev/tty", 0);

    /* Open a true-color workstation
     * System will be in state (PHOP,WSOP,STCL,ARCL) */
    popenws (WS_ID, 0, PWST_OUTPUT_TRUE);

    /* Open a structure to contain the output primitive.
     * System will be in state (PHOP,WSOP,STOP,ARCL) */
    popenstruct (STRUCT_ID);

    /* Create polyline attributes */
    create_polyline_attributes ();

    /* Create polyline primitive */
    create_polyline ();

    /* Close the structure containing the polyline primitive.
     * System will be in state (PHOP,WSOP,STCL,ARCL) */
    pclosestruct ();

    /* Post the structure to the open workstation */
    ppoststruct (WS_ID, STRUCT_ID, priority);

    /* Redraw all structures posted to the workstation -
     * This is the command which begins traversal of the
     * structure network (in this case a single structure) */
    predrawallstruct (WS_ID, PALWAYS);
```

```
    /* Sleep a while to let operator see the display */
    sleep (5);

    /* Close the workstation
     * System will be in state (PHOP,WSCL,STCL,ARCL) */
    pclosews (WS_ID);

    /* Close PHIGS
     * System will be in state (PHCL,WSCL,STCL,ARCL) */
    pclosephigs ();
}




create_polyline_attributes ()
{
#include <phigs.h>

    static Pint   line_colour = 2;
    static Pint   line_type  = 2;
    static Pfloat line_width  = 2.0;

    /* Set polyline color */
    psetlinecolourind (line_colour);

    /* Set the polyline type */
    psetlinetype (line_type);

    /* Set the polyline width */
    psetlinewidth (line_width);
}
```

Review Questions

1. What PHIGS functions are available to the application program if PHIGS is closed?

2. When PHIGS is opened. what tables are created and how are they initialized?

3. When a workstation is opened, what tables are created and how are they initialized?

4. Using Programming Example 1.1 as a starting point, write a PHIGS program that opens a second workstation. Make this workstation a pseudo color output workstation that is double-buffered.

5. When is a structure traversed? How is a structure traversed?

6. When a structure is reopened, where is the element pointer pointing? What effect does this have on new structure elements added to the structure?

7. Using Programming Example 1.2 as a starting point, write a PHIGS program that creates the triangle described below.

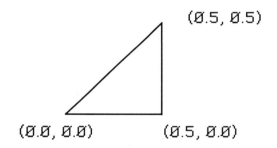

8. When is a structure drawn on a display surface?

9. Can a structure be drawn on more than one workstation at a time?

10. Write a PHIGS program that draws the structure you created in question (7) on the workstation created in Example Program 1.1. Write a PHIGS program the draws that same structure on both the workstations you created in question (4).

11. Using the PHIGS program you created in question (10), write a PHIGS program that creates a polyline output primitive with a line-type 4.

12. Using the PHIGS program you created in question (10), write a PHIGS program that creates a polyline output primitive with a linewidth scale factor of 4. Try the same program with a line type of 4.

2
Coordinate Systems and Transformations

Introduction

PHIGS is useful for displaying geometric data from a variety of sources because it allows the user to define an object in whatever coordinate space is most convenient. An object may be defined in angstrom units, inches, meters, light years, or any system that suits the application. The units of measure chosen are defined within a *modeling coordinate system* using the applicable measurements. PHIGS transforms the objects defined within the modeling coordinate system to physical locations on the graphics output device. These locations are within the *device coordinate system*. The process of conversion between the user-defined modeling coordinate system to the device coordinate system is known as the *transformation pipeline.*

The transformation pipeline is an ordered sequence of transformations that convert modeling coordinates to device coordinates. Figure 2.1 graphically presents the stages of the transformation pipeline. As shown in the figure, local modeling coordinates are input to the transformation pipeline. Structures are defined in local modeling coordinates. The coordinates of all the structures created by the application program are mapped into one unified coordinate space, the *world coordinate space.*[8] We define our view into the world coordinate space by creating a *view orientation*. The view orientation transformations convert the world coordinates to *view reference coordinates*, which are coordinates specified in relation to our view.

Section 2.1 deals with the local modeling transformation, stage of the transformation pipeline. PHIGS provides the application program with local transformations that perform translation, rotation, and scale within the local coordinate space. Section 2.1 will provide an example to demonstrate the translation local transformation.

---

[8]The process by which the local modeling coordinates are mapped into world space is discussed in more detail in Section 3.1.

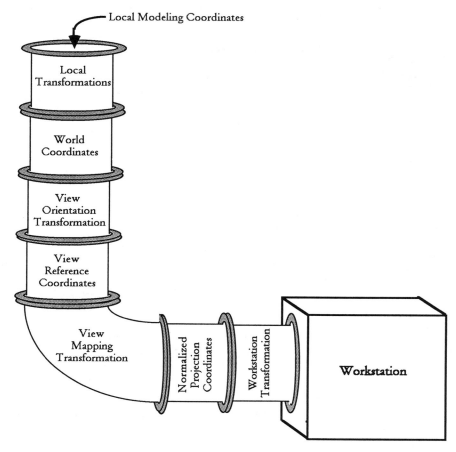

Figure 2.1. Transformation pipeline.

Transformations are based on matrix operations. We can combine transformation matrices so that one transformation operation will perform multiple transformations. Section 2.2 will discuss how transformation matrices are combined.

While local transformations refer to the orientation of a specific structure, a *view transformation* refers to the orientation of the viewing of the world space in which the structure exists. This process involves the creation of a *view representation*. PHIGS allows a software engineer to build a table of view representations, which is called the *view table*. To access this table, a *view index* must be set. Section 3.3 will discuss these concepts and demonstrate how a view is defined.

2.1 Modeling Transformations

When we describe an output primitive in a PHIGS structure we use *local modeling coordinates*. These coordinates are convenient to the application and are workstation independent. It is a simple matter, for example, to calculate the coordinates of a 4 X 4 square parallel to the X axis and whose lower left hand corner is at point (4, 5). The four corners of the square would be: (4, 5); (8, 5); (8, 9); and (4, 9). The coordinates defining an output primitive are not always so easy to calculate, however. What if the square were not parallel to the X axis, but rose 30° to the X axis? We can change the orientation, size, or location of an object by applying a *transformation*. Transformations convert, or transform, the output primitive's endpoint coordinates to a new set of coordinates specified by the application program. When we perform these operations on output primitives in the immediate structure we are performing *local transformations.*

One way to transform an output primitive is to transform individually each of the endpoint's coordinates. To rotate each corner of the square described above, we would perform the following calculations four times, once for each corner of the square:

$$X' = X \; cos\theta \; - \; Y \; sin\theta,$$
$$Y' = Y \; cos\theta \; + \; X \; sin\theta,$$

where

$$X', Y' = \text{transformed coordinate.}$$

Applying these calculations would result in the following:

Coordinate (5, 4)	Coordinate (8, 5)
4 * 0.87 - 5 * 0.5 = 0.96	8 * 0.87 - 5 * 0.5 = 4.42
5 * 0.87 + 4 * 0.5 = 6.33	5 * 0.87 + 8 * 0.5 = 8.33

Coordinate (8, 9)	Coordinate (4, 9)
8 * 0.87 - 9 * 0.5 = 2.42	4 * 0.87 - 9 * 0.5 = -1.03
9 * 0.87 + 8 * 0.5 = 11.79	9 * 0.87 + 4 * 0.5 = 9.79

This method is sufficient for this simple example, but, for each coordinate, we must perform six operations (one addition, one subtraction and four multiplications). We can, however, perform the transformation of the coordinate in a single concise operation by using a *transformation matrix.* To apply a transformation matrix to a coordinate, the coordinate vector[9] is multiplied by the transformation matrix. The following equations are used to translate, rotate and scale a 2-D coordinate. While it may be useful to know these equations, it is not necessary when working with PHIGS. As we shall see in the sections to follow, the contents of these matrices are not visible to the PHIGS programmer because

---

[9]In this context, the term *vector* refers to a single-dimensional array.

PHIGS will build these matrices and perform the necessary matrix multiplications. They are included here only for completeness.

$$(X', Y', 1) = (X, Y, 1) \begin{Bmatrix} 1 & 0 & 0 \\ 0 & 1 & 0 \\ T_X & T_Y & 1 \end{Bmatrix}$$

where

X', Y' = translated coordinate

$$(X', Y', 1) = (X, Y, 1) \begin{Bmatrix} \cos\theta & \sin\theta & 0 \\ \sin\theta & \cos\theta & 0 \\ 0 & 0 & 1 \end{Bmatrix}$$

where

X', Y' = rotated coordinate

$$(X', Y', 1) = (X, Y, 1) \begin{Bmatrix} S_X & 0 & 0 \\ 0 & S_Y & 0 \\ 0 & 0 & 1 \end{Bmatrix}$$

where

X', Y' = scaled coordinate.

When performing a two-dimensional transformation, we create a vector of three elements and a 3X3 *homogeneous transformation matrix*. The matrix is termed a homogeneous transformation matrix because no constant is required for its definition. Whenever we wish to apply a transformation matrix, we create a matrix and a coordinate vector that have one dimension more than the coordinate space with which we are working. After the transformation has been performed the extra dimension is discarded. As shown in Table 2.1, a 3-D transformation matrix is a 4X4 homogeneous transformation matrix. The reason for the creation of the added dimension deals with some of the fundamentals of mathematical techniques and coordinate geometry that are beyond the scope of this book.

To perform a coordinate transformation in PHIGS, we set the *local modeling transformation* to a user-created transformation matrix. The local modeling transformation matrix is applied to the output primitives that follow in the structure.[10] This transformation is applied until it is replaced or modified by the application program.[11] Applying this to our 4X4 square, we first create a 30°

---

[10]As we shall see in Chapter 3, local modeling transformations apply to subordinate structures in a structure network.

[11]In the examples in Chapter 1, we accepted the default local transformation, in PHIGS, the default local transformation is the identity transformation. The

rotation transformation matrix and then create our polyline. When we create the polyline we use the coordinates (4, 5), (8, 5), (8, 9), and (4, 9). The local transformation matrix will rotate it 30°.

Table 2.1. Three-dimensional transformation matrices.

Translate
$$\begin{Bmatrix} 1 & 0 & 0 & 0 \\ 0 & 1 & 0 & 0 \\ 0 & 0 & 1 & 0 \\ T_X & T_Y & T_Z & 1 \end{Bmatrix}$$

Scale
$$\begin{Bmatrix} S_X & 0 & 0 & 0 \\ 0 & S_Y & 0 & 0 \\ 0 & 0 & S_Z & 0 \\ 0 & 0 & 0 & 1 \end{Bmatrix}$$

Rotation around the Z-axis
$$\begin{Bmatrix} \cos\theta & -\sin\theta & 0 & 0 \\ \sin\theta & \cos\theta & 0 & 0 \\ 0 & 0 & 1 & 0 \\ 0 & 0 & 0 & 1 \end{Bmatrix}$$

Rotation around the Y-axis
$$\begin{Bmatrix} \cos\theta & 0 & \sin\theta & 0 \\ 0 & 1 & 0 & 0 \\ -\sin\theta & 0 & \cos\theta & 0 \\ 0 & 0 & 0 & 1 \end{Bmatrix}$$

Rotation around the Z-axis
$$\begin{Bmatrix} 1 & 0 & 0 & 0 \\ 0 & \cos\theta & -\sin\theta & 0 \\ 0 & \sin\theta & \cos\theta & 0 \\ 0 & 0 & 0 & 1 \end{Bmatrix}$$

identity transformation does not change the value of the coordinates specifying the output primitive.

Structure   **Resultant output**

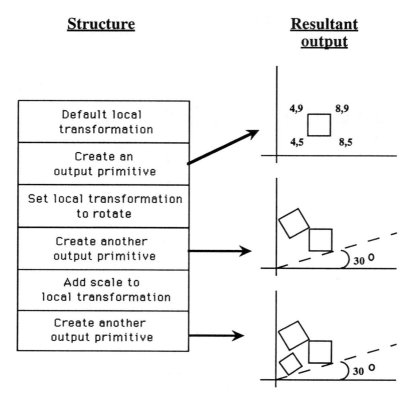

Figure 2.2. Local transformations.

Figure 2.2 demonstrates how the local transformation is applied to output primitives. When accepting the default identity transformation the output primitive's coordinates are not modified by the transformation. We set the local transformation to a rotation matrix by the transformation attribute, *set local transformation*, which is a structure element. After the local transformation has been set to rotate 30°, the output primitives that follow in the structure are rotated 30°. When the local transformation is modified to add scaling by the creation of another transformation attribute, the output primitives that follow in the structure are scaled and rotated 30°.

In Programming Example 2.1, we expand our view from two dimensions to three. There is a 2- and 3-D version of each PHIGS primitives. The 3-D polyline primitive is ppolyline3. The data structures passed to the 3-D primitive functions are named in similar manner. The data structure Ppoints3 is passed to ppolyline3. In a 2-D primitive, Z is assumed to be 0. For example the 3-D equivalent to the 2-D ppolyline function used in Programming Example 1.3 is ppolyline3. Function calls such as popenphigs and popenws are not affected by the number of dimensions. You will see these differences when examining Programming Example 2.1.

Programming Example 2.1

Programming Example 2.1 begins by opening PHIGS, a workstation, and a structure. After the structure has been opened, the program initializes a translation vector from which it creates a transformation matrix. This matrix is then set as the local transformation. It is very important to note that only when the transformation matrix is added to the structure that an actual structure element is created. Neither the initialization of translation vector nor the construction of the transformation matrix create structure elements.

Creation of the Transformation Matrix

The example program initializes the translation vector to tell PHIGS how far in the X, Y, Z direction we want the output primitive to be translated (moved). The translation vector is of type Pvector3 which is defined in phigs.h as:

```
typedef struct {
      Pfloat x;
      Pfloat y;
      Pfloat z;
}   Pvector3;
```

Our example initializes our translation vector to (0.15, 0.15, 0.00). This vector will be used to translate (move) the subsequent output primitives, 0.15 units along the X axis, 0.15 units along the Y axis, and 0.00 units along the Z axis. The translation vector is used as input to the PHIGS function, ptranslate3.

The following PHIGS function call to ptranslate3 creates the 4X4 homogeneous translation transformation matrix named trans_matrix:

```
ptranslate3
   (&trans_vector, &error_ind, trans_matrix);
                          /*(PHOP, *, *, *) */
```

The output of ptranslate3, trans_matrix, will be used as an input to the PHIGS function, psetlocaltran3, which sets the local transformation structure element. The transformation matrix is of type Pmatrix3, which is defined in phigs.h as `typedef Pfloat Pmatrix3 [4][4]`. The error indicator, error_ind, returns 0 if no error is detected. At this point, the application programmer may include error handling code.

Note the required state for the ptranslate3 function call. Since creating a matrix does not create a structure element, it does not matter if a structure or workstation is open. Here, we can begin to get a feel for why certain PHIGS states are required. When an operation does not interact with a workstation, the workstation need not be open. If the operation does not create a structure element or perform an operation on a structure, there is no need to have a structure open. *STOP AND THINK ABOUT THIS*. As you become more familiar with PHIGS, this will become more clear.

Set the Local Transformation

After we have created our transformation matrix, we are ready to set the local transformation. The following PHIGS function call will create an attribute that sets the local transformation to the translation transformation matrix named trans_matrix:

```
psetlocaltran3 (trans_matrix, PREPLACE);
                /*(PHOP,*,STOP,*) */
```

The local transformation is applied to subsequent output primitives. Any output primitives created by the example program after this attribute has been added to the structure will be translated to 0.15X, 0.15Y, and 0.00Z.

The second parameter to the function, *compose_type*, determines how the transformation matrix, trans_matrix, is combined with the current local transformation matrix. Compose type is defined within phigs.h as an enumeration type with the possible values of PPRECONCATENATE, POSTCONCATENATE, or PREPLACE. The PREPLACE mode, which is used in the example, replaces the previous transformation matrix with the transformation matrix that is passed as input to psetlocaltran3. There are times, however, when we may not wish to replace, but rather, to combine the current transformation matrix with the transformation matrix that is being passed to psetlocaltran3. The PPRECONCATENATE and PPOSTCONCATENATE modes specify how the current transformation matrix and the input transformation matrix are combined to form a new local transformation matrix.

Transformation matrices are combined through matrix multiplication. Unlike multiplication of scalar values,[12] multiplication of matrices is not commutative, matrix_a X matrix_b ≠ matrix_b X matrix_a. When multiplying the input transformation matrix with the current local transformation matrix, we must tell PHIGS how we want the two multiplied. The following lists how the different types of composition effect the output matrix:

Compose type	Operation
PREPLACE	N <= I
PPRECONCATENATE	N <= L X I
PPOSTCONCATENATE	N <= I X L

where

---

[12]A scalar variable is an individual value. An integer, a floating-point, or a fixed-point variable are all examples of scalar variables. This is in contrast to a single-dimensional array, which is a vector.

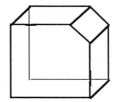

Figure 2.3. Example structure.

N = new transformation matrix,
L = current local transformation matrix, and
I = input transformation matrix.

The create_object subroutine creates the polyline output primitives and sets the attributes for the primitives. This subroutine creates the 3-D object shown in Figure 2.3. An important difference between the examples in Chapter 1 and Programming Example 2.1 is the use of multiple output primitives. Every time we invoke the ppolyline3 function, PHIGS creates a new output primitive. We do not, however, need to create any new structure attributes such as line color or type, since the attributes will not change until the application program changes them. Neither do we create a new transformation matrix; the local transformation matrix defined above will apply to all subsequent output primitives until it is modified or replaced by the application program.

After the object has been created, the structure is closed in the main program with a call to the PHIGS function pclosestruct. The example continues by posting the structure to the workstation and then drawing all structures. After the structure is made visible, the program sleeps to allow the operator to see the structure. The program then terminates by closing the workstation and PHIGS.

```
/*
 *                              Example 2.1
 */

#include <phigs.h>
#define     WS_ID             1
#define     STRUCT_ID         1

main()
{
    Pmatrix3        trans_matrix;
    Pvector3        trans_vector;
    Pint      error_ind;
```

```
/* Open PHIGS */
popenphigs ("/dev/tty", 0);

/* Open a true-color workstation */
popenws (WS_ID, 0, PWST_OUTPUT_TRUE);

/* Open a structure */
popenstruct (STRUCT_ID);

/* Create a translation vector  this is the x, y,
 * and z distance you wish to move the object */
trans_vector.x = 0.15;
trans_vector.y = 0.15;
trans_vector.z = 0.00;

/* Generate a 3D transformation matrix - note:
 * this DOES NOT create a structure element */
ptranslate3 (&trans_vector,&error_ind,trans_matrix);

/* An error handling routine could go here to check
 * the status of the error indicator. */

/* Set the matrix as the local transformation matrix
 * Note: This DOES create a structure element. The
 * PREPLACE flag is from the enumeration file and
 * means to replace the previous local trans-
 * formation matrix (in this case there was none) */
psetlocaltran3 (trans_matrix, PREPLACE);

/* Create the object */
create_object ();

/* Close the structure */
pclosestruct ();

/* Post the structure to the workstation */
ppoststruct (WS_ID, STRUCT_ID, 0.0);

/* Redraw all structures posted to the workstation */
predrawallstruct (WS_ID, PALWAYS);

/* Sleep awhile to let operator see object */
sleep (5);
```

```
    /* Close the workstation */
    pclosews (WS_ID);

    /* Close PHIGS */
    pclosephigs ();
}


create_object ()
{
#include <phigs.h>

    Ppoint3   side_1_vertex[6];
    Ppoint3   side_2_vertex[5];
    Ppoint3   side_3_vertex[6];
    Ppoint3   side_4_vertex[5];
    Ppoint3   side_5_vertex[5];
    Ppoint3   side_6_vertex[5];
    Ppoint3   side_7_vertex[5];

    /* initialize side 1 vertices */
     side_1_vertex[0].x =  0.4;
     side_1_vertex[0].y =  0.4;
     side_1_vertex[0].z =  0.1;
     side_1_vertex[1].x =  0.6;
     side_1_vertex[1].y =  0.4;
     side_1_vertex[1].z =  0.1;
     side_1_vertex[2].x =  0.6;
     side_1_vertex[2].y =  0.5;
     side_1_vertex[2].z =  0.1;
     side_1_vertex[3].x =  0.5;
     side_1_vertex[3].y =  0.6;
     side_1_vertex[3].z =  0.1;
     side_1_vertex[4].x =  0.4;
     side_1_vertex[4].y =  0.6;
     side_1_vertex[4].z =  0.1;
     side_1_vertex[5].x =  side_1_vertex[0].x;
     side_1_vertex[5].y =  side_1_vertex[0].y;
     side_1_vertex[5].z =  side_1_vertex[0].z;

    /* initialize side 2 vertices */
     side_2_vertex[0].x =  0.6;
     side_2_vertex[0].y =  0.4;
     side_2_vertex[0].z =  0.1;
     side_2_vertex[1].x =  0.6;
```

```
        side_2_vertex[1].y =  0.4;
        side_2_vertex[1].z = -0.1;
        side_2_vertex[2].x =  0.6;
        side_2_vertex[2].y =  0.5;
        side_2_vertex[2].z = -0.1;
        side_2_vertex[3].x =  0.6;
        side_2_vertex[3].y =  0.5;
        side_2_vertex[3].z =  0.1;
        side_2_vertex[4].x =  side_2_vertex[0].x;
        side_2_vertex[4].y =  side_2_vertex[0].y;
        side_2_vertex[4].z =  side_2_vertex[0].z;

    /* initialize side 3 vertices */
        side_3_vertex[0].x =  0.4;
        side_3_vertex[0].y =  0.4;
        side_3_vertex[0].z = -0.1;
        side_3_vertex[1].x =  0.6;
        side_3_vertex[1].y =  0.4;
        side_3_vertex[1].z = -0.1;
        side_3_vertex[2].x =  0.6;
        side_3_vertex[2].y =  0.5;
        side_3_vertex[2].z = -0.1;
        side_3_vertex[3].x =  0.5;
        side_3_vertex[3].y =  0.6;
        side_3_vertex[3].z = -0.1;
        side_3_vertex[4].x =  0.4;
        side_3_vertex[4].y =  0.6;
        side_3_vertex[4].z = -0.1;
        side_3_vertex[5].x =  side_3_vertex[0].x;
        side_3_vertex[5].y =  side_3_vertex[0].y;
        side_3_vertex[5].z =  side_3_vertex[0].z;

    /* initialize side 4 vertices */
        side_4_vertex[0].x =  0.4;
        side_4_vertex[0].y =  0.4;
        side_4_vertex[0].z = -0.1;
        side_4_vertex[1].x =  0.4;
        side_4_vertex[1].y =  0.4;
        side_4_vertex[1].z =  0.1;
        side_4_vertex[2].x =  0.4;
        side_4_vertex[2].y =  0.6;
        side_4_vertex[2].z =  0.1;
        side_4_vertex[3].x =  0.4;
        side_4_vertex[3].y =  0.6;
        side_4_vertex[3].z = -0.1;
```

```
 side_4_vertex[4].x =   side_4_vertex[0].x;
 side_4_vertex[4].y =   side_4_vertex[0].y;
 side_4_vertex[4].z =   side_4_vertex[0].z;

/* initialize side 5 vertices */
 side_5_vertex[0].x =   0.4;
 side_5_vertex[0].y =   0.6;
 side_5_vertex[0].z =   0.1;
 side_5_vertex[1].x =   0.5;
 side_5_vertex[1].y =   0.6;
 side_5_vertex[1].z =   0.1;
 side_5_vertex[2].x =   0.5;
 side_5_vertex[2].y =   0.6;
 side_5_vertex[2].z =  -0.1;
 side_5_vertex[3].x =   0.4;
 side_5_vertex[3].y =   0.6;
 side_5_vertex[3].z =  -0.1;
 side_5_vertex[4].x =   side_5_vertex[0].x;
 side_5_vertex[4].y =   side_5_vertex[0].y;
 side_5_vertex[4].z =   side_5_vertex[0].z;

/* initialize side 6 vertices */
 side_6_vertex[0].x =   0.4;
 side_6_vertex[0].y =   0.4;
 side_6_vertex[0].z =   0.1;
 side_6_vertex[1].x =   0.6;
 side_6_vertex[1].y =   0.4;
 side_6_vertex[1].z =   0.1;
 side_6_vertex[2].x =   0.6;
 side_6_vertex[2].y =   0.4;
 side_6_vertex[2].z =  -0.1;
 side_6_vertex[3].x =   0.4;
 side_6_vertex[3].y =   0.4;
 side_6_vertex[3].z =  -0.1;
 side_6_vertex[4].x =   side_6_vertex[0].x;
 side_6_vertex[4].y =   side_6_vertex[0].y;
 side_6_vertex[4].z =   side_6_vertex[0].z;

/* initialize side 7 vertices */
 side_7_vertex[0].x =   0.5;
 side_7_vertex[0].y =   0.6;
 side_7_vertex[0].z =   0.1;
 side_7_vertex[1].x =   0.6;
 side_7_vertex[1].y =   0.5;
 side_7_vertex[1].z =   0.1;
```

```
side_7_vertex[2].x =   0.6;
side_7_vertex[2].y =   0.5;
side_7_vertex[2].z =  -0.1;
side_7_vertex[3].x =   0.5;
side_7_vertex[3].y =   0.6;
side_7_vertex[3].z =  -0.1;
side_7_vertex[4].x =   side_7_vertex[0].x;
side_7_vertex[4].y =   side_7_vertex[0].y;
side_7_vertex[4].z =   side_7_vertex[0].z;

/*set the line color index attribute structure element*/
psetlinecolourind (1);

/*create a polyline primitive structure element for
 *each side */
ppolyline3 (6, side_1_vertex);
ppolyline3 (5, side_2_vertex);
ppolyline3 (6, side_3_vertex);
ppolyline3 (5, side_4_vertex);
ppolyline3 (5, side_5_vertex);
ppolyline3 (5, side_6_vertex);
ppolyline3 (5, side_7_vertex);
}
```

2.2 Matrix Composition

In the previous section, we learned how to perform a transformation by creating
a transformation matrix. We then used this matrix to set the local transformation.
This section will demonstrate how to combine matrices to perform a series of
transformations. In Programming Example 2.1, we performed a simple
translation. How do we perform a translation and a rotation? Or, how do we
perform rotations around more than one axis?

Matrix Composition combines multiple transformation matrices into a single
matrix. In the previous section, we saw how a local transformation may be
composed of several transformation matrices by pre or postconcatenation. In this
section we will create a transformation matrix that will perform a rotation
around the X, Y, and Z axes. To perform these transformations we will first
create a transformation matrix for each of the rotations. These matrices will then
be combined into one transformation matrix, which will be used as our local
transformation matrix.

Programming Example 2.2

Programming Example 2.2 opens PHIGS and a workstation. It then creates three transformation matrices, one matrix for rotation about each axis. The example demonstrates how these matrices are combined into one transformation matrix that will perform all three rotations. This matrix is then set as the local transformation matrix. After the structure has been displayed on a workstation, the program will delete the structure and use the same structure ID to create a new structure with a different local transformation.

Rotation

As shown in Table 2.1, rotation around each of the axes requires their own rotation transformation matrix. We create each of the matrices by specifying the angle of rotation for each axes, with the following PHIGS function calls:

```
protatex(angle_x, &error_ind, x_matrix);
protatey(angle_y, &error_ind, y_matrix);
protatez(angle_z, &error_ind, z_matrix);
      /*(PHOP,*,*,*)*/
```

The function receives, as input, the angle of rotation about the axes specified in radians. A positive value indicates a clockwise rotation, a negative value indicates a counterclockwise rotation. In the example program, we have set the angle_x, angle_y, and angle_z variables to 0.1 radians. These variables are defined as a floating point.

Each of the functions return an error indicator and transformation matrix. If no error is detected the function returns a 0. The returned transformation matrices are 4X4 homogeneous transformation matrices, which perform the rotation by the specified angle *about the origin*. The transformation matrix is of type Pmatrix3. We will use each of these matrices to compose a single transformation matrix.

It is important to note that the rotation is about the origin and not a point specified by the application program. Figure 2.4a demonstrates the effect of rotation about the origin. We use a simple 2-D polyline here to demonstrate the concept, although the principles being demonstrated apply to 3-D rotation as well. In Figure 2.4 we rotate a polyline output primitive 30°. We see that the first coordinate of the polyline is transformed from (5, 5) to (1.83, 6.83). The figure accompanying these data reflects this transformation.

Figure 2.4b demonstrates the same rotation as in Figure 2.4a, but this time the rotation is about the point (5, 5) instead of the origin. In order to rotate an output primitive around a specific point, we must first translate the output primitive to the origin, perform the rotation, and then translate the output primitive back to its original position The first step of the process translates the output primitive so that point (5, 5) is at the origin. Next we rotate the output primitive 30°. We

Polygon 1 Coordinates	Polygon 2 Coordinates
(5,5)	(1.8, 6.8)
(8,5)	(4.4, 8.3)
(8,7)	(3.4, 10.0)
(7,8)	(2.0, 10.0)
(5,8)	(0.3, 9.4)

Figure 2.4a. Rotation about the origin.

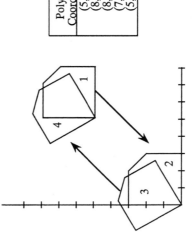

Polygon Coordinates	Translated Coordinates	Rotated Coordinates	Translated Coordinates
(5, 5)	(0,0)	(0,0)	(5,5)
(8, 5)	(3,0)	(2.5,1.5)	(7.5,6.5)
(8, 7)	(3,2)	(1.5,3.2)	(6.5,8.2)
(7, 8)	(2,3)	(0.2,3.5)	(8.2,8.5)
(5, 8)	(0,3)	(-1.5, 2.6)	(3.5,7.5)

Figure 2.4b. Rotation about a point.

then translate the output primitive so that the origin is at point (5, 5). Using this process, we can rotate the output primitive around any point.

Matrix Composition

The individual transformation matrices can now be used to compose a transformation matrix that rotates around all three axes. We begin with the X and Y rotation transformation matrices. The example program uses the following PHIGS function call to perform the multiplication:

```
pcomposematrix3
    (X_matrix,Y_matrix,&error_ind,temp_matrix);
                 /*(PHOP,*,*,*)*/
```

Remember that matrices are composed through matrix multiplication, which is not commutative. The pcomposematrix3 function multiplies the first matrix by the second, that is to say, `temp_matrix <= X_matrix   X Y_matrix`. The review questions of this chapter experiment with composing matrices in different orders.

The output of this function is the error indicator, error_ind, and the transformation matrix, temp_matrix. The error indicator is set to 0 if there is no error. The transformation matrix is of the type `Pmatrix3`, which is defined in phigs.h.

We multiply the temp_matrix and the Z-rotation transformation matrix to create our final transformation matrix. The program performs this composition with the following function call:

```
pcomposematrix3
    (temp_matrix,z-matrix,&error_ind,rotate_matrix);
                 /*(PHOP,*,*,*)*/
```

The output of this function call, rotate_matrix, is then passed as input to the psetlocaltran3 function. This function, as described in Section 2.1, will use the input transformation matrix, rotate_matrix, to replace the previous local transformation. It is not until we have replaced the current transformation matrix with rotate_matrix that an attribute structure element is created.

After the local transformation has been set, the program calls create_object to create the output primitives. The example program then closes the structure and posts it to the workstation. Once the structure is drawn on the workstation, the program sleeps to allow the operator to observe the display.

Unposting and Deleting the Structure

When we discussed posting a structure to a workstation, we noted that the structure remains posted to that workstation until it is specifically unposted, deleted, or the workstation is closed. The following PHIGS function unposts the structure identified by STRUCT_ID from the workstation WS_ID:

```
punpoststruct (WS_ID, STRUCT_ID);
                        /*(PHOP,WSOP,*,*)*/
```

When a structure is unposted, it is no longer displayed on the workstation. How soon after the function call this change takes effect depends on the update state of the workstation (refer to Chapter 1). Although the structure is no longer posted to the workstation, it still exist within the CSS. This means that the unposted structure is available for posting to another workstation or for editing.

Deleting a Structure

The structure is not removed from the CSS until it is specifically deleted by the application program. The following PHIGS function deletes the structure identified by STRUCT_ID from the CSS:

```
pdelstruct (STRUCT_ID);      /*(PHOP,*,*,*)*/
```

A structure that is closed during deletion is simply removed from the CSS. If the structure is open at the time it is deleted, PHIGS closes the structure, deletes it from the CSS, and creates a new structure with the same structure ID.

Scaling a Structure

Since the matrix created by the pcomposematrix3 function call is not a structure element, the deletion of the structure, which was open at the time of its creation, does not effect the matrix. The matrix still exist within memory. To demonstrate that the matrix is independent of the structure, the example continues by multiplying the rotate_matrix with a scale matrix.

First, we initialize a scaling vector that is of the type Pmatrix3. In the example program, we have initialized each element of this vector to 0.5. A scale factor of 1.0 has no effect on the structure, a scale factor of 0.5 is one-half the size. Since the factor for all three axes is the same, the structure will retain its original proportions. At times, the application program may wish to set the scale factor on the axes to different values in order to modify the proportions of the structure.

A structure may also seem to change the relative position of a structure. When a structure is scaled the entire axis is scaled, not just the coordinates of the structure. Actually, the position of the structure has not changed since the coordinates are the same, the axis has been condensed. If, for example, a scale factor of 0.2 is applied to the X-axis the structure may seem to shift to the left-hand side. Really, the X axis, has been scaled back 80% of its original distance.

The following PHIGS function call creates a scale transformation matrix from the input scale vector, scale_vector:

```
pscale3
    (&scale_vector,&error_ind,scale_matrix);
                        /*(PHOP,*,*,*)*/
```

The function outputs the error indicator, error_ind, and the scale transformation matrix, scale_matrix.

The function pcomposematrix3 is used to multiply the rotation matrix created earlier by the scale matrix. The current local transformation matrix is then replaced with the rotate and scale transformation matrix. The program then creates the same output primitives which were created above and closes the structure.

The new structure is posted to the workstation and all structures posted to that workstation are redrawn. Since this structure is the only structure posted to the workstation, it is the only structure redrawn. The program sleeps to allow the operator to see the newly posted structure. Note the difference between this structure and the structure that was drawn on the workstation earlier in the program. After the program wakes from the sleep, it terminates after closing the workstation and PHIGS.

```c
/*
 *                           Example 2.2
 */
#include <phigs.h>

#define      WS_ID                   1
#define      STRUCT_ID               1

main()
{
    Pint            error_ind;
    Pfloat          angle_x, angle_y, angle_z;
    Pmatrix3        x_matrix, y_matrix, z_matrix;
    Pmatrix3        rotate_matrix;
    Pmatrix3        scale_matrix;
    Pmatrix3        temp_matrix;
    Pmatrix3        matrix;
    Pvector3        scale_vector;

    /* Open PHIGS */
    popenphigs ("/dev/tty", 0);

    /* Open a true-color workstation */
    popenws (WS_ID, 0, PWST_OUTPUT_TRUE);

    /* Open a structure */
    popenstruct (STRUCT_ID);
```

```
/* Set rotation angles - Remember,
 * rotation is relative to the origin */
angle_x = 0.2;
angle_y = 0.2;
angle_z = 0.2;

/* Create x, y and z rotation matrices */
protatex(angle_x, &error_ind, x_matrix);
protatey(angle_y, &error_ind, y_matrix);
protatez(angle_z, &error_ind, z_matrix);

/* Generate a matrix composed of the x and y matrices */
pcomposematrix3
        (x_matrix, y_matrix, &error_ind, temp_matrix);

/* Generate a matrix composed of the x & y and
 * z matrices */
pcomposematrix3
   (temp_matrix,z_matrix,&error_ind,rotate_matrix);

/* Set the matrix as the local transformation matrix */
psetlocaltran3 (rotate_matrix, PREPLACE);

/* Create the object */
create_object ();

/* Close the structure */
pclosestruct ();

/* Post the parent structure */
ppoststruct (WS_ID, STRUCT_ID, 0.0);

/* Redraw all structures posted to the workstation */
predrawallstruct (WS_ID, PALWAYS);

/* Sleep awhile so operator can see display */
sleep (5);

/* Unpost the structure */
punpoststruct (WS_ID, STRUCT_ID);

/* Delete the structure - This is one way to reuse
 * a structure with new data */
pdelstruct (STRUCT_ID);
```

```
/* Open a new structure - Use the old structure
 * identification */
popenstruct (STRUCT_ID);

/* Set the scale factors - Note: 1.0 is normal, 0.5 is
 * half size */
scale_vector.x = 0.5;
scale_vector.y = 0.5;
scale_vector.z = 0.5;

/* Create the scale matrix */
pscale3 (&scale_vector,&error_ind,scale_matrix);

/* Generate a matrix composed of the x, y and
 * z matrices created above with the scale matrix
 * this is possible because the calls to create matrices
 * do not create structure elements.  The matrix is
 * still in main memory */
pcomposematrix3
      (rotate_matrix, scale_matrix, &error_ind, matrix);

/* Set the matrix as the local transformation matrix */
psetlocaltran3 (matrix, PREPLACE);

/* Create the object */
create_object ();

/* Close the structure */
pclosestruct ();

/* Post the parent structure */
ppoststruct (WS_ID, STRUCT_ID, 0.0);

/* Redraw all structures posted to the workstation */
predrawallstruct (WS_ID, PALWAYS);

/* Sleep awhile so operator can see display */
sleep (5);

/* Close the workstation */
pclosews (WS_ID);

/* Close PHIGS */
pclosephigs ();
}
```

2.3 Viewing Transformations

In Chapter 1 we presented workstations as abstractions of a graphic device; in this section, we will describe an output workstation a bit differently. Consider, for a moment, the world coordinate space we discussed in Section 2.2. In this space, we have many structures existing in many different locations within this space. Think of the world coordinate space for a moment as a totally separate universe from our own. Everything in this universe is created by our application program. When we want to see anything, we must define a view portal into this universe. The output workstation is our portal into this alternate reality. Through this portal, we can view the world in whichever way we decide is most appropriate for our application.

In all the previous examples, we simply accepted whatever the PHIGS default view was for our workstation. If we wanted to view the object from the different perspectives shown in Figure 2.5, we would have to translate and rotate the entire structure to fit this view. An alternative to changing the location of the scene is to change our view of the scene.

A scene is viewed through *projections*. Projections take an object in three dimensions and transforms it to two dimensions (i.e., a flat display surface). Although projections can be applied to viewing any multidimensional object in fewer than the number of original dimensions, this discussion deals with viewing three dimensions in two. In a projection, we take what is in a 3-D space and project it onto a 2-D *projection plane*. The location from which we view this projection is called the *projection reference point* (PRP). From the PRP extend two projectors which are the outermost edges of the view. In other words, the projectors are the limits of our peripheral vision.

There are two types of projections, *perspective* and *parallel*. The projectors in a perspective projection are not parallel. The point at which the two lines meet is the perspective reference point. In a parallel projection, the projectors are parallel. The perspective reference point is, therefore, located at infinity, since all parallel lines meet at infinity. Figure 2.6 graphically shows the difference between the two types of projections.

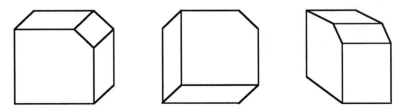

Figure 2.5. Viewing structure from different perspectives.

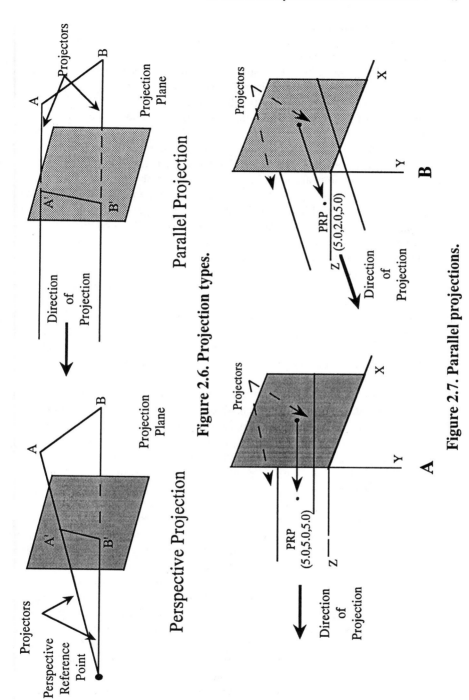

Parallel Projection

Perspective Projection

Figure 2.6. Projection types.

Figure 2.7. Parallel projections.

In PHIGS, the PRP is used to determine the direction of the projection. The projectors in a parallel projection are parallel to a vector that is drawn from the center of the window to the PRP. As we said above, in a parallel projection the PRP is at infinity. We, therefore, specify a point between infinity and the window as our PRP in the parallel projection to specify the direction of the projection. In Figure 2.7a we have a parallel projection with a PRP of (5.0, 5.0, 5.0). The center of the window is at point (5.0, 5.0, 0.0). The projectors for this projection are, therefore, parallel to the Z axis. In Figure 2.7b we have presented the same projection, but the PRP has been moved to (5.0, 2.0, 5.0). The projectors for this projection approach the window at an angle to the Z axis.

Perspective projections are useful in environments where realistic scenes are to be created. If we want to project something on a display that would resemble our view of the real world, we would use a perspective projection. Parallel projections are most useful in scientific work. When a parallel projection is used, the relative distances between points remain the same regardless of the distance from the PRP. This is useful in some scientific applications.

The closer we get to the center of the projection the larger objects become and, conversely, the farther away we get from the center of the projection the smaller objects become. Just as objects that are too close to our eyes obscure our vision and objects too far are indistinguishable, objects that are too close to the perspective reference point obscure our view and objects that are too far are too small to see. To eliminate these problems, we define a front clipping plane and a back clipping plane to our view. Objects outside of these planes are *clipped* from the view.

The clipping planes, projection reference point, and view plane all define the *viewing volume* as shown in Figure 2.8. Everything within the view volume is projected onto the view plane. We take the front clipping plane and project everything between it and the view plane onto the view plane, in short "flattening" everything from the front plane back onto the view plane. We then do the same with the back plane. The following example program will take us through each of these steps.

It is important to understand how the front and back planes relate to what we see on the display. In Figure 2.9 we have shown a cross-section of a view volume. Within the view volume, we have two spheres of equal size. When the spheres are viewed from the PRP in perspective projection, the sphere closer to front plane appears larger than the sphere near the back plane. Remember what projections do, they take everything in a 3-D view volume and project it onto a 2-D plane. Everything between the front plane and view plane must be enlarged in order to map onto the larger window on the view plane. Thus, objects between the front plane and view plane appear larger. Everything between the view plane and the back plane is shrunk and flattened in order to map onto the smaller window on the view plane. Thus, objects between the view plane and back plane appear smaller. Just as in the real world, objects that are closer to the eye appear larger than objects of the same size that are farther away from the eye. Objects

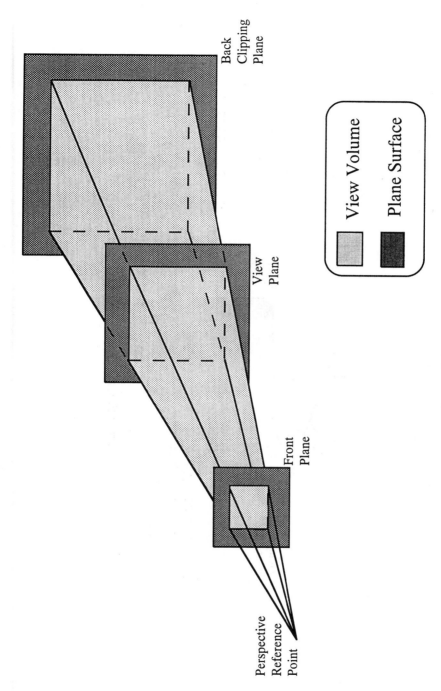

Figure 2.8. View volume.

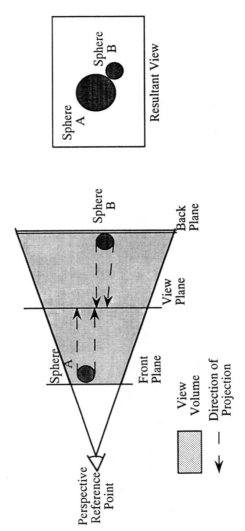

Figure 2.9. Cross section of view volume.

on the front plane which are closer to the PRP appear larger than objects on the back plane, which are farther away from the PRP.

Programming Example 2.3

Example Program 2.3 is the same as Example Program 2.2 with the exception of a call to the user subroutine, define_view, after the workstation is opened in the main program. The define_view subroutine creates a view and enters it into the workstation view table. Once the structure is opened, the program creates a structure element that is an index to the view table. The program also calls the user subroutine, create_axis, which builds a structure that defines an axis. The axis is displayed on the workstation to orient each of the successive displays of the object. Since the remainder of the program is the same as what has been discussed in Section 2.2, we will begin our review of the example program in the define_view subroutine.

Evaluate the View Orientation Matrix

The first step in the building of a view volume is the orientation of the *view reference coordinate system* (VRC). The view reference coordinate system is a device-independent three-dimensional Cartesian coordinate system in which the parameters for the view-mapping transformation are specified. The axes of the VRC system are called U, V, N axes. We orient this coordinate system by telling PHIGS where this system exists in relation to the world coordinate system. We first tell PHIGS where the origin of the system is located and, then, in which direction each of the axes (U, V, N) are pointing.

Once PHIGS understands where the VRC system exists in relation to the world coordinate system, it can build a view orientation matrix. If we refer to the transformation pipeline presented in Figure 2.1, we see that the view orientation transformation converts world coordinates (XYZ coordinates) to view reference coordinates (UVN coordinates). By creating the VRC system, we are describing to PHIGS where we are looking. We are creating a reference coordinate system that is oriented to our view. The following PHIGS function sets up the view orientation transformation matrix for the view reference coordinate space:

```
pevalvieworientationmatrix3
 (&vrp,&vpn,&vup,&err,rep.orientation_matrix);
                          /*(PHOP,*,*,*)*/
```

The first parameter to the function call, vrp, is the *view reference point*, which is the origin of the view reference coordinate system. The parameter vrp is of type Ppoint3. We specify the location of the view reference point in world coordinates. In the example program, we have set the view reference point to (0.0, 0.0, 0.0) in the world coordinate system. This places the origin of the view reference coordinate system at the origin of the world coordinate system.

The second parameter to the function call, vpn, is of type Pvector3. The line from the view reference point to the point specified by VPN describes the N axis of the view reference coordinate system. The *view plane* is parallel to the plane formed by the U-V axes of the view reference coordinate system. Since the N axis is a normal[13] to the view plane, the N axis is often referred to as the *view plane normal*. Imagine nailing a clear square of plexiglass to the end of a pole; the plexiglass is our view plane, and the pole is the N axis. We then place the end of the pole that is opposite the plexiglass at the end of our nose so that it always points in the direction we are looking. This is what we are doing in PHIGS when we specify the VPN and the VRP. We are telling PHIGS where in the world space the pole (N axis) is located and which way it is pointing. It is onto this plane that our view volume is ultimately projected.

When we specify the VPN, we use world coordinates that are relative to the VRP. The values we use to define the VPN, therefore, are offsets to the coordinates of the VRP. In Figure 2.10a we have defined a view reference point of (3.0, 1.0, 0.0) and a view plane normal (VPN) to be (0.0, 0.0, 1.0). The world coordinate of a point on the normal is (3.0, 1.0, 1.0). This creates a view plane that is parallel to the X, Y plane of the world coordinate space. In Figure 2.10b we have defined a VPN to be (0.0, -2.0, 0.0) with the same VRP. The world coordinate of a point on the normal is now (3.0, -2.0, 0.0). This has created a view plane that is parallel to Z, X plane of the world coordinate space. We can also create planes that are not parallel to the world coordinate axes by defining a VPN that is not parallel to a world coordinate axes, as we demonstrate in Figure 2.10c. The VPN was specified as (-3.0, -1.0, 1.0). When the offset is applied to the VRP, we find the point (00, 0.0, 1.0) is on the normal. This puts the view plane at an angle to the Y Z plane of the world coordinate space. In the example program, we have defined the view plane normal, VPN, to be (0.0, 0.0, 1.0) in world coordinates. The N axis of the view reference coordinate system is, therefore, the Z axis of the world coordinate system. This makes the view plane parallel to the plane that is formed by the X-Y plane in the world coordinate system. We have demonstrated this in Figure 2.10d.

The third parameter to this function call, vup, specifies the *view up vector*.[14] This parameter is of type Pvector3 and is defined in world coordinates relative to the view reference point. The view-up vector describes the direction of the V axis, basically, it is telling PHIGS which way is up. The view reference coordinate system's V axis is defined as an orthogonal projection of the view-up vector onto the view plane through the view reference point and perpendicular to the view plane normal. Vectors parallel to the view-up vector in world coordinate space will appear vertical in the final image.

In Figure 2.11 we have shown the effect different view-up vector values have on a single image. The first position of the view up vector is set to (0.0, 1.0, 0.0). As the V value of a coordinate increases, the coordinate moves closer to the top of the screen. When the view up vector is to (1.0, 0.0, 0.0), the positive U values proceed to the top of the screen. Another way to think of this is that the

---

[13]A line that is perpendicular to a plane is called a *normal* to the plane.
[14]This is referred to, in some circles, as the LeResche vector.

coordinate system is rotated counter clockwise 90°. The reverse would be setting the view-up vector to (-1.0, 0.0, 0.0) which would cause the negative U values to proceed to the top of the screen, or the image is rotated clockwise 90°.

Let us return to our pole analogy for a moment. If we set the VUP to (0.0, 1.0, 0.0), we are standing on our feet looking forward. If we set the VUP to (1.0, 0.0, 0.0), we have rotated around the pole to the left until we are lying on our right hand side. If VUP is set to (-1.0, 0.0, 0.0), we are rotated to the right until we are lying on our left hand side. A VUP of (0.0, -1.0, 0.0) would have us standing on our head with a pole at the end of our nose. It is not recommended by the authors that you attempt these exercises.

The view reference point, view-up vector, and the view plane normal fully describe the view reference coordinate system. The VPN defines the N axis of the view reference coordinate system. Since the N axis is a normal to the U-V plane, the N axis also defines the view plane orientation. The view up vector defines the V axis. The U axis is perpendicular to the V axis in the view plane, so it does not need to be further specified by the application program. *STOP AND THINK ABOUT THIS.*

The output of this function call is rep.orientation_matrix which is of type Pmatrix3. This is a 4X4 homogeneous view orientation transformation matrix. It is later used in the example program as input for defining the view representation function.

Evaluate the View Mapping Matrix

The next step in setting up the view is to generate a view-mapping transformation matrix. Referring to Figure 2.1, we see that the view mapping transformation transforms points in VRC to points in the *Normalized Projection Coordinate (NPC)* system. The NPC system is a device-independent three-dimensional Cartesian coordinate system in which the composition of images is specified to the graphics system. The view-clipping limits and the workstation window is defined in NPC space.

We create the view-mapping matrix by specifying the location of the front plane, view plane and back plane of the view volume and the window of the view volume. The input parameter, mapping, passes these data to the PHIGS function that creates the matrix. The following PHIGS function creates the mapping matrix:

```
pevalviewmappingmatrix3
          (&mapping,&err,rep.mapping_matrix);
                    /* (PHOP, *, *, *) */
```

The function returns the view-mapping matrix, rep.mapping_matrix, and an error indicator. The rep.mapping_matrix data structure is defined as Pmatrix3. This is a 4X4 homogeneous transformation matrix containing the view-mapping matrix. It is later used in the example program as input for defining the view representation function.

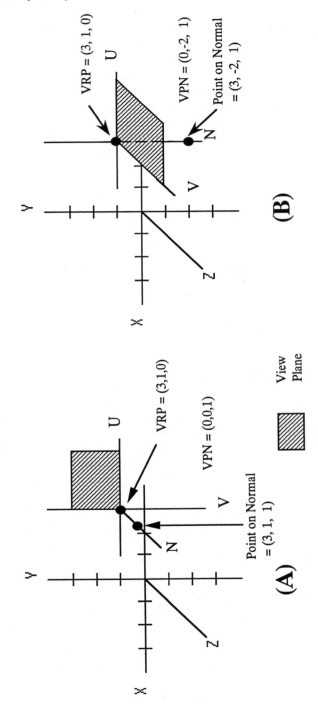

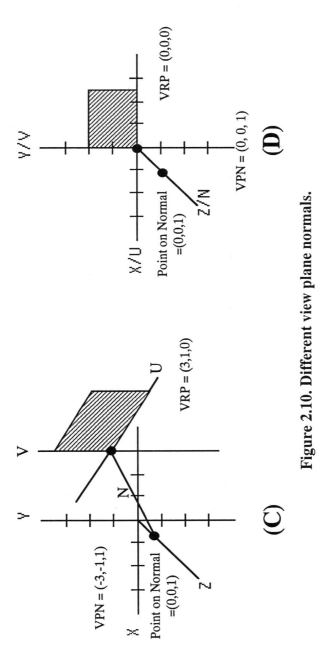

Figure 2.10. Different view plane normals.

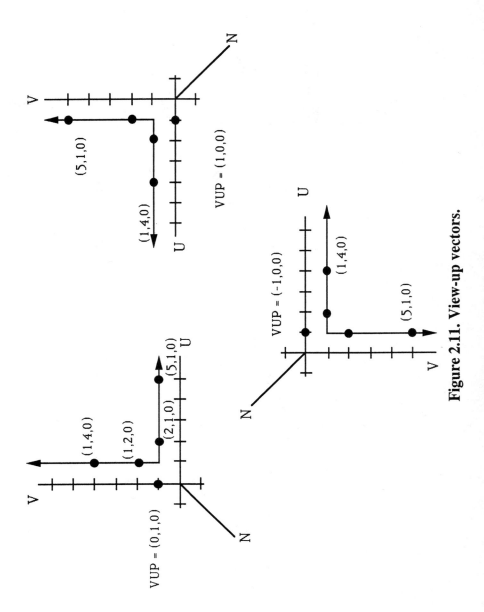

Figure 2.11. View-up vectors.

The input parameter, mapping, is of type Pviewmapping3. This data structure is defined in phigs.h as follows:

```
typedef struct {
      Plimit    window;         /* VRC window limits
      Plimit3   viewport;       /* NPC viewport limits */
      Pprojtype proj;           /* projection type to be
                                   applied in NPC */
      Ppoint3   prp;            /* projection ref. point */
      Pfloat    view_plane;     /* view plane   */
      Pfloat    back_plane;     /* back plane   distance */
      Pfloat    front_plane;    /* front plane distance */
} Pviewmapping3;
```

The example program defines the location of each of the planes in the view volume. The view_plane data element is a floating point value containing the N coordinate through which the view plane passes. This coordinate is specified as a distance along the N axis from the VRP. In the example we have used the value 0.0. This makes the U-V plane of the UVN coordinate system the view plane. The back clipping plane and front clipping plane distances specify the number of units along the N axis between each of theses planes and the view plane. In the example, we have used a 1.0 for the front plane, and a -1.0 for the back plane. As we can see in Figure 2.12, the view plane passes through the origin. The front plane passes through point (0.0, 0.0, 1.0), while the back plane passes through point (0.0, 0.0, -1.0). Both the front and back plane are parallel to the view plane.

The *projection reference point* is defined in phigs.h as type Ppoint3. When the view volume is created with a perspective projection, projectors are drawn from the projection reference point through the front plane to the back plane. If the projection type is parallel, the projectors are parallel and cross at infinity.[15] The projectors pass through the view plane at the corners of the view window, which is defined by the window component of the mapping data structure. The window structure is defined in phigs.h as follows:

```
typedef struct {
      Pfloat    xmin;     /* X minimum */
      Pfloat    xmax;     /* X maximum */
      Pfloat    ymin;     /* y minimum */
      Pfloat    ymax;     /* y maximum */
} Plimit;
```

The view window marks the top, bottom, and sides of the view volume. As we see in Figure 2.12 the projectors extend from the projection reference point to the view plane at the corners of the window defined by the lower left (XMIN, YMIN) and upper right-hand corners (XMAX, YMAX). These projectors extend

---

[15]All parallel lines meet at infinity.

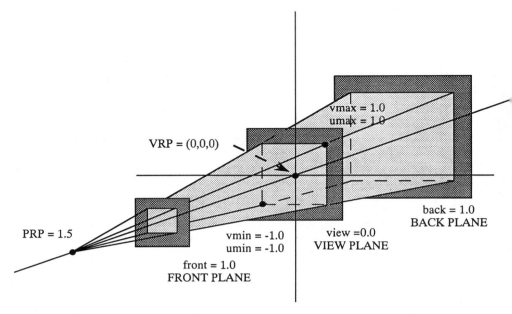

Figure 2.12. Perspective view volume created by example.

to the back plane, defining three windows, one in each of the planes through which they pass. Everything contained within the view volume, is projected onto the window on the view plane. This is shown in Figure 2.12.

The projector component of the mapping data structure defines the type of projection we want to use for this view. The projection type is an enumerated type that can have one of two values: PPARALLEL or PPERSPECTIVE. This example uses the perspective projection.

The *viewport* component of the mapping data structure defines the viewport in the normalized projection space. This viewport defines the min/max X, Y, Z values in NPC space into which the VRC coordinates are mapped. The viewport component is defined in phigs.h as

```
typedef struct {
    Pfloat    xmin;     /* X minimum */
    Pfloat    xmax;     /* X maximum */
    Pfloat    ymin;     /* y minimum */
    Pfloat    ymax;     /* y maximum */
    Pfloat    zmin;     /* z minimum */
    Pfloat    zmax;     /* z maximum */
} Plimit3;
```

Setting the View Representation

Let us stop and review what we have done so far. We first created the view orientation matrix which transforms the world coordinates to VRC space. Remember that we have defined VRC space in relation to our view of the world. The next step defined a view mapping matrix which projects the VRC space onto the view plane. With both of the matrices created, we are ready to define the view representation for our workstation. When we define this view we insert it into the workstation view table with the following PHIGS function call:

```
psetviewrep3(ws_id,view_index,&rep);
                      /*(PHOP,WSOP,*,*)*/
```

The first parameter to the function call is the identification of the workstation to which the view is assigned. This workstation must be open at the time this function is called. The second parameter to the function is the view table index. Later, a structure that is to use this view uses the index as a reference. The size of the view table is implementation-dependent. View number 0 is the identity transformation encompassing all of the NPC space cube and cannot be changed. Table entry 0 is shown in Table 2.2.

The third parameter to the function call is the new view representation that is to be added to the view table. This data structure is of type Pviewrep3, which is defined in phigs.h as follows:

```
typedef struct {
  Pmatrix3 orientation_matrix;   /*orientation matrix */
  Pmatrix3 mapping_matrix;       /*mapping matrix */
  Plimit3      clip_limit;       /* Clipping limits */
  Pclip        clip_xy           /* X-Y clipping Ind. */
  Pclip        clip_back         /* Clip back */
  Pclip        clip_front        /* Clip front */
} Pviewrep3;
```

Table 2.2. View table entry 0 define view.

Orientation Matrix		Identity Matrix
Mapping Matrix		Identity Matrix
View Clipping Limits		
Xmin/Xmax		0.0/1.0
Ymin/Ymax		0.0/1.0
Zmin/Zmax		0.0/1.0
X-Y Clipping Indicator	Clip	
Front Plane Clipping	Clip	
Back Plane Clipping	Clip	

The first two components of this data structure are the matrices we created earlier in this section. The clip_limit, which is of type Plimit3, defines the clipping limits of our view.

The next three components of the data structure turn clipping on or off for each of their respective dimensions. These components are of type Pclip which is an enumeration type defined in PHIGS. These variables may be set to either Pclip or Pnoclip. Clipping is performed by the limits that are set by clip limit. In the example program we have turned clipping off.

If a structure exceeds the bounds of the view volume, the portion of the structure that exceeds those bounds will be clipped, regardless of the setting of the clip flags. In our example, we have defined the clip_limits to be at the front and back clipping planes. If, for example, we have defined the clip limits to be 0.25 to -0.75N and drew a sphere with its center at (3.0, 3.0, 0.0) and a radius of three, the sphere would be clipped at 0.25 and 0.75N with clipping turned on. If we then turned clipping off, the sphere would be clipped at 1.0 and 0.0N. The only way to display the entire sphere is to set the front planes to 3.0 and the back plane to -3.0 or more. Of course we would also have to adjust the size of the view window to allow the entire sphere to fit in the U-V dimensions as well.

The subroutine, define_view, returns control to the calling program after the call to psetviewrep3. The main program, as it had in previous examples, creates the local transformation matrices and output primitives. After the structure is created, it is posted to a workstation where it is drawn. The program terminates after the workstation and PHIGS have been closed.

Setting the View Index

When creating a structure we can select any view defined for that workstation. Different structures posted to the same workstation can use different views. The following PHIGS function selects a view to display a structure:

```
psetviewind (VIEW_ID);        /*(PHOP,*,STOP,*)*/
```

The function receives as input an integer value that is an index value into the workstation's view table. The function creates a structure element that is an attribute defining the view of all subsequent output primitives.

```
/*
 *
 */                              Example 2.3
#include <phigs.h>

#define    WS_ID        1
#define    STRUCT_ID    1
#define    VIEW_ID      1
```

```
main()
{
    Pint          error_ind;
    Pfloat        angle_x, angle_y, angle_z;
    Pmatrix3      x_matrix, y_matrix, z_matrix;
    Pmatrix3      rotate_matrix;
    Pmatrix3      scale_matrix;
    Pmatrix3      temp_matrix;
    Pmatrix3      matrix;
    Pvector3      scale_vector;

    /* Open PHIGS */
    popenphigs ("/dev/tty", 0);

    /* Open a true-color workstation */
      popenws (WS_ID, 0, PWST_OUTPUT_TRUE);

    /* Define a view - This defines a view and
     * assigns its parameters to a workstation
     *    view table */
    define_view (WS_ID, VIEW_ID);

    /* Open a structure */
    popenstruct (STRUCT_ID);

    /* Set the view index This creates a structure
       * element referencing a view defined on the
       * workstation view table */
    psetviewind (VIEW_ID);

    /* Create an axis */
    create_axis ();

    /* Set rotation angles Remember, rotation is
     * relative to the origin */
    angle_x = 0.2;
    angle_y = 0.2;
    angle_z = 0.2;

    /* Create x, y, and z rotation matrices */
    protatex (angle_x, &error_ind, x_matrix);
    protatey (angle_y, &error_ind, y_matrix);
    protatez (angle_z, &error_ind, z_matrix);
```

```
/* Generate a matrix composed of the
 *           x and y matrices */
pcomposematrix3
        (x_matrix, y_matrix, &error_ind, temp_matrix);

/* Generate a matrix composed of the x & y and
 * z-matrices */
pcomposematrix3
        (temp_matrix, z_matrix, &error_ind,
         rotate_matrix);

/* Set the matrix as the local
 *           transformation matrix */
psetlocaltran3 (rotate_matrix, PPRECONCATENATE);

/* Create the object */
create_object ();

/* Close the structure */
pclosestruct ();

/* Post the parent structure */
ppoststruct (WS_ID, STRUCT_ID, 0.0);

/* Redraw all structures posted
 *      to the workstation */
predrawallstruct (WS_ID, PALWAYS);

/* Sleep a while so operator can see display */
sleep (5);

/* Unpost the structure */
punpoststruct (WS_ID, STRUCT_ID);

/* Delete the structure */
pdelstruct (STRUCT_ID);

/* Open a new structure */
popenstruct (STRUCT_ID);

/* Set the view index */
psetviewind (VIEW_ID);
```

```
/* Create an axis */
create_axis ();

/* Set the scale factors Note: 1.0 is normal,
 * 0.5 is half size */
scale_vector.x = 0.5;
scale_vector.y = 0.5;
scale_vector.z = 0.5;

/* Create the scale matrix */
pscale3 (&scale_vector, &error_ind, scale_matrix);

/* Generate a matrix composed of the x, y,
 * and z-matrices created above with the scale
 * matrix */
pcomposematrix3
        (rotate_matrix, scale_matrix, &error_ind, matrix);

/* Set the matrix as the local transformation matrix */
psetlocaltran3 (rotate_matrix, PPRECONCATENATE);

/* Create the object */
create_object ();

/* Close the structure */
pclosestruct ();

/* Post the parent structure */
ppoststruct (WS_ID, STRUCT_ID, 0.0);

/* Redraw all structures posted to the workstation */
predrawallstruct (WS_ID, PALWAYS);

/* Sleep a while so operator can see display */
sleep (5);

/* Close the workstation */
pclosews (WS_ID);

/* Close PHIGS */
pclosephigs ();
}
```

```
create_axis ()
{
#include <phigs.h>

    Ppoint3         x_axis_vertex[2];
    Ppoint3         y_axis_vertex[2];
    Ppoint3         z_axis_vertex[2];

    Pchar           x_text[1];
    Pchar           y_text[1];
    Pchar           z_text[1];
    Ppoint3         x_points[1];
    Ppoint3         y_points[1];
    Ppoint3         z_points[1];
  static Pvector3   dir[2] = {{1,0,0},{0,1,0}};
  static Pvector3   ar = {1.0, 1.0, 1.0};
  static Pfloat     expan = 1.0;
  static Pfloat     space = 0.0;
  static Pfloat     height = 0.05;
  static Pvector    upvec = {0.0, 1.0};
  static Ptxpath    path = {PTP_RIGHT};
  static Ptxalign   align ={PAH_CENTRE,PAV_HALF};

  /* initialize x-axis vertices */
  x_axis_vertex[0].x =  0.0;
  x_axis_vertex[0].y =  0.0;
  x_axis_vertex[0].z =  0.0;
  x_axis_vertex[1].x =  0.2;
  x_axis_vertex[1].y =  0.0;
  x_axis_vertex[1].z =  0.0;

  /* initialize y-axis vertices */
  y_axis_vertex[0].x =  0.0;
  y_axis_vertex[0].y =  0.0;
  y_axis_vertex[0].z =  0.0;
  y_axis_vertex[1].x =  0.0;
  y_axis_vertex[1].y =  0.2;
  y_axis_vertex[1].z =  0.0;

  /* initialize z-axis vertices */
  z_axis_vertex[0].x =  0.0;
  z_axis_vertex[0].y =  0.0;
  z_axis_vertex[0].z =  0.0;
  z_axis_vertex[1].x =  0.0;
```

```
        z_axis_vertex[1].y =   0.0;
        z_axis_vertex[1].z =   0.2;

        /* set the line color index attribute
           * structure element*/
        psetlinecolourind (2);

        /* create a polyline primitive structure
         * element for each axis */
        ppolyline3 (2, x_axis_vertex);
        ppolyline3 (2, y_axis_vertex);
        ppolyline3 (2, z_axis_vertex);

        x_points[0].x = 0.25;
        x_points[0].y = 0.00;
        x_points[0].z = 0.00;
        y_points[0].x = 0.00;
        y_points[0].y = 0.25;
        y_points[0].z = 0.00;
        z_points[0].x = 0.00;
        z_points[0].y = 0.00;
        z_points[0].z = 0.25;

        /* set text attributes */
        psetcharexpan(expan);        /*character expansion */
        psetcharspace(space);        /*character spacing */
        psetcharheight(height);      /*character height */
        psetcharup(&upvec);          /* up vector */
        psettextpath(path);          /* text path */
        psettextalign(&align);       /* text alignment */
        psettextcolourind(2);
        ptext3(&x_points, dir, "X");
        ptext3(&y_points, dir, "Y");
        ptext3(&z_points, dir, "Z");
}


define_view(ws_id, view_index)
int ws_id, view_index;
{
#include <phigs.h>

        static Ppoint3f      vrp    = { 0.25, 0.25, 0.00};
        static Ppoint3f      vpn    = { 0.00, 0.00, 1.00};
        static Ppoint3f      vup    = { 0.00, 1.00, 0.00};
```

```
static Ppoint3f      prp     = { 0.00, 0.00, 2.00};
static Plimit        window  = {-0.50, 1.00, -0.50, 1.00};
static Plimit3       viewport = { 0.00, 1.00, 0.00, 1.00,
                                  0.00, 1.00};
static Pfloat        back  =  -0.50;
static Pfloat        view  =   0.00;
static Pfloat        front =   1.00;
Pviewrep3            rep;
Pviewmapping3 mapping;
Pint                 err;

/* Calculate view orientation matrix for
 * SET VIEW REPRESENTATION */
pevalvieworientationmatrix3
   (&vrp,&vpn,&vup,&err,rep.orientation_matrix);

/* Define view mapping data */
mapping.window       = window;
mapping.viewport     = viewport;
mapping.proj = PPARALLEL;
mapping.prp   = prp;
mapping.view_plane   = view;
mapping.back_plane   = back;
mapping.front_plane      = front;

/* Generate 3-D transform matrix to project VRC
 * window to NPC viewport */
pevalviewmappingmatrix3
        (&mapping,&err, rep.mapping_matrix);

/* Define boundaries of area in NPC space which can
 * be displayed. These are the cliping limits.
 * An object which passes through a plane 1/4 of the way
 * in may be clipped by setting zmax to 0.75 */

rep.clip_limit.xmin =  0.0;
rep.clip_limit.ymin =  0.0;
rep.clip_limit.zmin =  0.0;
rep.clip_limit.xmax =  1.0;
rep.clip_limit.ymax =  1.0;
rep.clip_limit.zmax =  1.0;

/* Disable X, Y and Z clipping */
rep.clip_xy          = PNOCLIP;
rep.clip_back        = PNOCLIP;
```

```
rep.clip_front        = PNOCLIP;

/* Define 3-D view representation
 * entry on workstation view table */
psetviewrep3 (ws_id, view_index, &rep);
}
```

Review Questions

1. What is the transformation pipeline? What is its purpose?

2. How many local transformations are there? What are they?

3. What is the structure and content of each of the transformation matrices?

4. Write a PHIGS program that performs a 30° rotation, and a scale using the create_object subroutine from Programming Example 2.1. Use postconcatenation to compose the matrices. After viewing the results, repeat the same exercise using preconcatenation.

5. What is a projection? Why is it called a "projection"?

6. How is the view plane normal defined?

7. Open a workstation and create a view table entry for each of the views presented in Figure 2.10. Post to that workstation the structure created in question 4. How do each of these views differ?

8. What is the purpose of the view-up vector?

9. Change the program created in question 5, so that each of the views in the view table uses a view up vector presented in Figure 2.11. How do each of these views differ?

10. How are the different axes of the UVN coordinate system defined? What is another name for the UVN coordinate system.

11. How are the front and back planes related to what is seen on the screen?

12. Using the program created above, repetitively change move the front and back plane closer to the view plane.

13. Using Example 2.3 as a starting point, modify the define_view subroutine to use a parallel projection. Experiment with different values for the PRP to see how it affects the image.

3
More on Structures

Introduction

This chapter will introduce some of the more dynamic capabilities provided by the hierarchical nature of PHIGS. On completion of this chapter the reader will be able to create multiple structures linked in a hierarchical manner. The reader will also be able to dynamically modify these structures in order to simulate motion.

As the name of the standard implies PHIGS is hierarchical. Structures are able to invoke other structures creating a hierarchy of structures known as *structures networks*. One advantage of a hierarchy is the ability to treat complex structures composed of many subordinate structures as a single structure. Section 3.1 deals with the use of such hierarchies. A PHIGS program will be provided that will demonstrate the creation of a structure network.

Throughout this chapter, it is demonstrated that structures are objects, objects that can be modified as well as invoked. We modify a structure by editing the structure. Section 3.2 discusses how elements within a structure may be labeled and indexed. Understanding networks will enable the user to move through the network using element labels and pointer offsets from those labels. An example program will be provided that will edit a structure.

Section 3.3 will bring together the ideas discussed in the two previous sections. This section discusses how dynamic motion is achieved through repetitively editing and displaying a structure.

3.1 Structure Hierarchies

One of the distinguishing features of the PHIGS standard is that it is hierarchical. We are given the ability to create hierarchies of structures known as *structure networks*. In a structure network a structure executes, or invokes, another structure. The structure that invoke another is a *parent structure* while the structure that was invoked is the *child structure*. A parent structure may in turn be invoked by another structure. The topmost structure of this network is referred to as the *root structure*.

Hierarchies provide the PHIGS programmer with several significant advantages. Primarily, hierarchies simplify graphics programs by performing much of the processing that would have to be performed by the application program. For example, without hierarchies if we wanted to spin a plate on the end of a stick and then move that stick the application program would have to maintain the position of the plate relative to the stick. As we shall see in the examples to follow, hierarchies relieve us of these concerns.

From a software engineering point of view, structure networks facilitate the use of an *object-oriented* approach[16] to graphics programming. The example program will demonstrate how a structure can be seen as an object. Associated with the object are operations such as transformations, which can act on these objects. In a very real sense, the structure becomes something, some object, that is processed, acted on, by the application program. Since a structure and a structure network are processed in the same way by PHIGS, we can see that individual complex objects (structure) can be composed of many simple subobjects (child structures).

Figure 3.1 demonstrates how a hierarchy can be used to create a complex structure. The figure shows a dual-limbed robotic arm extending from a base. If we create the arm so the structures that define the two limbs are children of the structure defining the base, when we rotate, translate, or scale the base, the two limbs will also be rotated, translated, and scaled. This structure demonstrates how neatly hierarchies relate to the real world. If the robotic arm were a physical object we wished to examine, we would take the arm by the base and turn it; the entire arm, limbs and all, would follow. In much the same way, this is what we do with a structure network, as we perform transformations on a parent structure, the children of the parent are transformed to maintain their original geometric relationships. *STOP AND THINK ABOUT THIS.*

Figure 3.1 also demonstrates how structure networks simplify our graphics program. We first create the structures for the basic elements of the graphics object, the base (a rectangle), the joint (a circle), and the hand (a pentagon). The parent structure then executes the base and the joint child structures. We then create the two limbs by executing the same child structure with a different local transformation. The limb structure executes the base and joint structures. *STOP AND THINK ABOUT THIS.* Programming Example 3.1 will demonstrate creating a simpler structure network.

---

[16]The reader is referred to Booch, G: Object-oriented development, IEEE Transactions on Software Engineering, vol. SE-12, no. 2, February 1986; and Nielson, K. and Shumate, K: *Designing Large Real-Time Systems with Ada,* McGraw-Hill, New York, 1988.

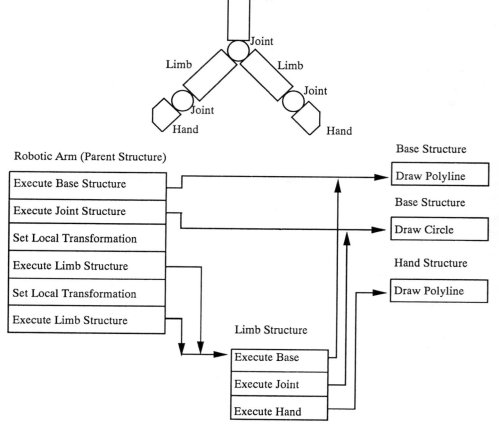

Figure 3.1. Structure hierarchy.

Programming Example 3.1

Programming Example 3.1 creates a simple structure network. The example starts by opening PHIGS, a workstation, and the parent structure. The parent structure of our network, identified by PARENT_ID, is the topmost structure in the network, therefore, it is the root structure. If the parent structure were to be executed later by another structure it would not be considered the root structure since it is a child to the structure that executes it.

After opening the parent structure, the example program sets the view index and local transformation matrix. The local transformation is set to translate the output primitives 0.15 in the X and Y. When we set a local transformation and a view index, we are creating an attribute in the parent structure. As is the case with most filial relationships, the child inherits the attributes of the parent.

In the previous chapter, we said the coordinates of all the structures created by the application program are mapped into one unified coordinate space, the *world coordinate space*. The mapping is performed by the structure's *Composite Modeling Transformation*, which is a composite of the local modeling transformation and the *global transformation*. The global transformation is the composite transformation which is inherited from the parent. The root structure's global transformation is set to the identity transformation. The global transformation is the modeling transformation that is in effect when the child structure is executed.

Figure 3.2 graphically demonstrates the relationship between the global coordinates that are established by the parent's composite transformation, and the local coordinates, which are used by the child. In the example, we perform a translation 0.15 in the X, and Y direction in the parent structure. This transformation matrix is concatenated with the parent's global transformation. For this example, we will assume it to be the identity matrix. This translates the coordinate system local to the child 0.15 in the X, and Y direction. When we describe the point (0.40, 0.40, 0.10) in local space, we are describing the point (0.55, 0.55, 0.10) in global space, as is shown in the figure.

Executing a Child Structure

After creating the view index and local transformation structure elements the example program executes the child structure. The following PHIGS function creates a structure element that will cause the child structure to be executed:

```
pexecutestruct (child_id);
                        /*(PHOP, *, STOP, *)*/
```

The function receives as input the ID of the child structure that is to be executed. The structure element that is created by this function contains the ID of the structure to be executed.

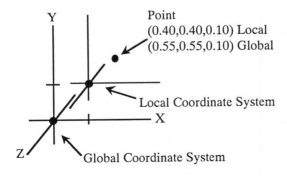

Figure 3.2. Global-local coordinates relationship.

When we execute a child structure, PHIGS suspends the traversal of the current structure and saves the state of the PHIGS traversal state list. The *global modeling transformation.* is set to the composite modeling transformation. The local transformation is then set to the identity transformation matrix. The child structure is then fully traversed. After the child has been traversed, the PHIGS state list prior to execution of the child is restored and traversal of the parent structure is resumed. If the child structure, in turn executes another structure (a grandchild of the parent), the traversal process is recursively performed until the bottom of the network is reached. Structures that are higher in the hierarchy than the parent structure, are said to be ancestors of the parent's child structures. In our robotic arm example, the root structure is an ancestor of the hand structure.

Earlier, we discussed how the child inherits the attributes of the parent. The parent, however, does *not* inherit the attributes of the child. If a child structure resets an attribute, such as color or local transformation, that attribute applies only to the structures that are subordinate to the child. In the example we have used the create_object subroutine used in Chapter 2. This subroutine sets the line color, width and style. When traversal returns to the parent structure, the attributes of the parent prior to the traversal of the child are restored. *STOP AND THINK ABOUT THIS.*

When traversal of the child structure is completed in the example program, the parent structure is closed and the child structure is opened for creation. Since the structure traversal does not occur when the structure is created, it is not necessary that the child structure be created prior to the parent. To create the child structure the example program calls the create_object subroutine, which was presented in Chapter 2. After the child has been created, the parent structure is posted to the workstation where it is drawn with the predrawallstruct PHIGS function call. This initiates traversal of the structure process. The example program sleeps to allow the user time to view the structure.

```
/*
 *                                     Example 3.1
 */
#include <phigs.h>

#define     WS_ID               1
#define     STRUCT_ID           1
#define     VIEW_ID             1
#define     CHILD_ID            2

main()
{
    Pmatrix3        trans_matrix;
    Pvector3        trans_vector;
    Pint            error_ind;
```

```
/* Open PHIGS */
popenphigs ("/dev/tty", 0);

/* Open a true-color workstation */
popenws (WS_ID, 0, PWST_OUTPUT_TRUE);

/* Define a view for the workstation */
define_view (WS_ID, VIEW_ID);

/* Open a parent structure */
popenstruct (STRUCT_ID);

/* Set the view index */
psetviewind (VIEW_ID);

/* Create an axis structure */
create_axis ();

/* Create a translation vector This is the x, y,
 * and z distance you wish to move the child
 * structure */
trans_vector.x = 0.15;
trans_vector.y = 0.15;
trans_vector.z = 0.00;

/* Generate a 3-D transformation matrix
 * Note: this DOES NOT create a structure
 * element */
ptranslate3
   (&trans_vector,&error_ind, trans_matrix);

/* An error handling routine could go here
 * to check the status of the error indicator.*/

/* Set the matrix as the local transformation
 * matrix - Note: This DOES create a structure
 * element. The PREPLACE flag is from the
 * enumeration file and means to replace
 * the previous local transformation matrix
 * (in this case there was none) */
psetlocaltran3 (trans_matrix, PREPLACE);

/* Execute the child structure The child structure will
 * be created later.  Nothing will be executed until the
 * structure network is traversed (using predrawallstruct
```

```
     * or pupdatews).  We cannot create child structure now
     * because we already have a structure open. When
     * executed, the child structure will inherit the above
     * transformation and view from the parent. */
    pexecutestruct (CHILD_ID);

    /* Close the structure */
    pclosestruct ();

    /* Open the child structure */
    popenstruct (STRUCT_ID);

    /* Draw the object */
    create_object ();

    /* Close the child structure */
    pclosestruct ();

    /* Post the parent structure to the workstation Note:
     * only the parent structure is posted.  The child
     * structure will be executed by the parent. */
    ppoststruct (WS_ID, STRUCT_ID, 0.0);

    /* Redraw all structures posted to the workstation */
    predrawallstruct (WS_ID, PALWAYS);

    /* Sleep awhile to let operator see object */
    sleep (5);

    /* Close the workstation */
    pclosews (WS_ID);

    /* Close PHIGS */
    pclosephigs ();
}
```

3.2 Structure Editing

In Chapter 1 we discussed the centralized structure store. All the structures stored in the CSS can be modified by *structure editing*. Remember that, structures are lists of structure elements. When editing a structure, the PHIGS programmer opens the structure to add, modify, or delete structure elements.

We edit a structure by establishing an *edit mode* prior to opening a structure. Once the structure is opened, we can then access any structure element by moving the *element pointer*. PHIGS does not allow us to change the value of the element pointer directly. Instead, we are provided a set of functions that will do it for us. Depending on the edit mode, we are able to replace structure elements pointed at by the element pointer or insert new structure elements after the element pointed at by the element pointer. The following example will demonstrate how we can replace structure elements in a structure.

Programming Example 3.2

Programming Example 3.2 demonstrates how editing is used to modify the contents of a structure. The example first creates the same structure network that was created in Programming Example 3.1. Programming Example 3.2, however, sets the local transformation matrix to the identity matrix. After the structure network is drawn on the workstation, the example program edits the parent structure. In the edit session, the example program replaces the parent's the local transformation matrix with a new transformation matrix.

Note that the example program initializes the translation matrix to the identity matrix. This is necessary in some implementations of PHIGS, although it is not required as part of the standard. Check your individual implementation for what is required.

Creating a Label

After the parent structure is opened, a *label* structure element is created. A label is a structure element containing a value label identifier. We create this label structure element so that it is one element before the set local transformation matrix structure element. It is inserted into a structure to identify a location within the structure. The following PHIGS function call is used to create a label structure element:

```
plabel (LABEL);              /*(PHOP,*,STOP,*)*/
```

The function receives as input an integer, which is the label identifier. We use this label as a pointer to the next element in the structure. When we open the structure later for editing, we will use this label to reset the element pointer. The value of the label need not be unique within the structure. PHIGS will sequentially search a structure for labels, the search will stop at at the first occurrence of the label.

After the label is inserted into the parent structure, the example program sets the local transformation matrix to the identity matrix. This is the transformation matrix that will be replaced during the edit session. The parent structure then executes the child structure and is closed. After the child structure is created, the parent structure is posted and drawn to the workstation. The program sleeps for five seconds to allow the user to view the object. The example program is then ready to edit the structure.

Setting the Edit Mode

Prior to editing a structure, an edit mode must be established. The edit mode tells PHIGS how structure elements are to be entered into the structure. The example program sets the edit mode with the following PHIGS function:

```
pseteditmode (PEDIT_REPLACE);
                                    /*(PHOP,*,*,*)*/
```

The function receives as input an integer value that specifies either REPLACE or INSERT. When edit mode is set to replace, a new structure element replaces the structure element that is pointed to by the element pointer. When edit mode is set to insert, new structure elements are inserted in to the structure after the element pointed to by the structure element pointer.

When we open the parent structure, the element pointer is pointing to the last element in the structure by default. To edit an existing structure element, we must first move the element pointer to the beginning of the structure. Remember that PHIGS will search from the current element pointer position until it finds a label or until the end of the structure, whichever comes first. It will not search backward.

Set the Element Pointer

To reset the element pointer to the beginning of the structure, we make the following PHIGS function call:

```
psetelemptr (0);                /*(PHOP,*,STOP,*) */
```

The function receives as input an integer value to be assigned to the element pointer. Element positions are numbered within the structure 0 to N, where element position 1 is the first element in the structure and position 0 is before the first element. If the input value is less than 0, the element pointer is set to 0. If the element pointer is set to a value which is greater than the number of elements in the open structure, the element pointer is set to point at the last element in the structure.

After the function call, the element pointer is pointing to the top of the structure. If we were to create a new structure element in insert mode, it would be the first in the structure. If, for example, we were to set a local transformation, it would be the first structure element. The element pointer would point to the structure element containing the set local transformation. Any new structure elements would be inserted into the structure after the newly created output primitive. In the example program, we want to go to where we put a label and start modifying the structure there.

Set the Element Pointer at the Label

When the structure was created, we put a label structure element in the structure for future reference. We will now use that label to reposition our pointer within the structure with the following PHIGS function call:

```
psetelemptrlabel (LABEL);
                         /*(PHOP,*,STOP,*) */
```

The function receives as input an integer value that is the label identifier. PHIGS sequentially searches the structure for the next occurrence of the specified label. The search begins at the current element pointer location and continues to the end of the structure. If the label is not found between the element pointer and the end of the structure, an error is generated. If the element pointer is already positioned at the label, the value of element pointer remains unchanged.

In the example program, we set the element pointer to the top of the structure (pointer value = 0) and then start the search. At first, this may seem a bit redundant, but remember that the search for the label is between the structure element currently pointed at by the element pointer and the the end of the structure. If we did not reset the element pointer to 0, the element pointer would be pointing at the end of the structure and the label would not be found.

Although we have positioned the element pointer to point at the label, this is not sufficient because we actually want to change the structure element that follows. If we were to create a new structure element at this point, the new structure element would replace the label and not the transformation matrix. Remember that the structure was opened in replace mode. We know that the local transformation matrix is one element beyond the label. To replace it, all we need do is increment the element pointer by 1, so that it points at the transformation matrix.

Offset the Element Pointer

Although PHIGS does not allow direct access to the element pointer, we are provided with a function that will modify it for us. The following function increments the element pointer by a specified value:

```
poffsetelemptr (1);    /*(PHOP,*,STOP,*) */
```

The function receives, as input, the offset to the current element pointer. The offset value is added to the current element pointer. If the resultant value is less than 0, the element pointer is set to 0. If the resultant value is set to a value that is greater than the number of elements in the structure that is open, the element pointer is set to point to the last element in the open structure. In the example program, the offset is 1. This will increment the element pointer by 1 causing it to point to the set local transformation structure element.

The example program creates a new transformation matrix, which will translate the structure 0.15 in the X and Y directions. It is then used to create a new set local transformation structure element. Since the edit session has started in replace mode, the new structure element replaces the set local transformation structure element. The example program then redraws all structures for the workstation to allow the user to observe the difference in the newly transformed structure.

After the structure has been redrawn, the program closes the structure, the workstation, and PHIGS. Note that after closing the structure the example program resets the edit mode to insert. While it may not be necessary to reset the edit mode, it is a good idea to develop a habit of so doing. In more complex programs, it is very easy to forget that you are in replace mode and unintentionally replace structure elements.

```
/*
 *                           Example 3.2
 */
#include <phigs.h>

#define     WS_ID               1
#define     STRUCT_ID           1
#define     VIEW_ID             1
#define     CHILD_ID            2
#define     LABEL               1

main()
{
    Pmatrix3        trans_matrix;
    Pvector3        trans_vector;
    Pint            error_ind;

    /* Open PHIGS */
    popenphigs ("/dev/tty", 0);

    /* Open a true-color workstation */
    popenws (WS_ID, 0, PWST_OUTPUT_TRUE);

    /* Define a view for the workstation */
    define_view (WS_ID, VIEW_ID);

    /* Open a parent structure */
    popenstruct (STRUCT_ID);

    /* Set the view index */
    psetviewind (VIEW_ID);
```

```
/* Create the axis */
create_axis ();

  /* Set a label - This serves as a pointer to
   * the following structure element */
plabel (LABEL);

/* Initialize translation matrix to identity (normal) -
 * No structure element is created, just a matrix in
 * main memory */
identity3 (trans_matrix);

/* Set the identity matrix as the local transformation
 * matrix - A structure element is created.  The label is
 * therefore just before this structure element.  Later
 * we will come back to edit this structure element
 * containing the set local transform element */
psetlocaltran3 (trans_matrix, PREPLACE);

/* Execute the child structure - The child structure will
 * be created later.  Nothing will be executed until the
 * structure network is traversed (using predrawallstruct
 * or pupdatews).  We cannot create child structure now
 * because we already have a structure open. When
 * executed, the child structure will inherit the above
 * transformation and view from the parent. */
pexecutestruct (CHILD_ID);

/* Close the structure */
pclosestruct ();

/* Open the child structure */
popenstruct (STRUCT_ID);

/* Draw the object */
create_object ();

/* Close the child structure */
pclosestruct ();

/* Post the parent structure to the workstation - Note:
 * only the parent structure is posted.  The child
 * structure will be executed by the parent. */
ppoststruct (WS_ID, STRUCT_ID, 0.0);
```

```
/* Redraw all structures posted to the workstation */
predrawallstruct (WS_ID, PALWAYS);

/* Sleep a while to let operator see object */
sleep (5);

/* Set edit mode to replace - This will put all
 * succeeding calls into the same place in DLM so that
 * just the one set local transformation instruction will
 * be changed (Note: a common mistake is to forget to
 * reset edit mode to INSERT before defining a new
 * structure, resulting in a structure which contains
 * nothing) */
pseteditmode (PEDIT_REPLACE);

/* Open the parent structure so it can be edited */
popenstruct (STRUCT_ID);

/* Set the element pointer to the beginning of the parent
 * structure - the pointer will be at the end of the
 * structure if you don't reset it to the beginning */
psetelemptr (0);

/* Set the element pointer to the label - This points to
 * the label, to replace the local matrix the pointer
 * will have to be offset to the next element in the
 * structure */
psetelemptrlabel (LABEL);

/* Offset the element pointer to point to the local
 * transformation */
poffsetelemptr (1);

/* Create a translation vector - This is the x-, y- and
 * z-distance you wish to move the child structure */
trans_vector.x = 0.15;
trans_vector.y = 0.15;
trans_vector.z = 0.00;

/* Generate a 3-D transformation matrix - Note: this DOES
 * NOT create a structure element */
ptranslate3 (&trans_vector, &error_ind, trans_matrix);
```

```
    /* Set the matrix as the local transformation matrix -
     * Note: this creates a structure element which replaces
     * the previous element to which the element pointer is
     * pointing */
    psetlocaltran3 (trans_matrix, PREPLACE);

    /* Redraw all structures posted to the workstation */
    predrawallstruct (WS_ID, PALWAYS);

    /* Close the structure that was open for editing - This
     * is often forgotten, creating a state error when trying
     * to open another structure */
    pclosestruct ();

    /* Set edit mode to replace - Although this it not
     * necessary in this example (as no more structure
     * creation will take place), it is a good idea to get
     * into the habit of always re-setting the edit
     * mode to insert (the default).  Forgetting to do so
     * will cause problems later in more complex programs.
     * You will be in a situation where every structure
     * element is overwritten, creating structures containing
     * nothing */
    pseteditmode (PEDIT_INSERT);

    /* Close the workstation */
    pclosews (WS_ID);

    /* Close PHIGS */
    pclosephigs ();
}


identity3 (m)
Pmatrix3            m;

{
m[0][0] = 1.0;  m[0][1] = 0.0;m[0][2] = 0.0;m[0][3] = 0.0;
m[1][0] = 0.0;  m[1][1] = 1.0;m[1][2] = 0.0;m[1][3] = 0.0;
m[2][0] = 0.0;  m[2][1] = 0.0;m[2][2] = 1.0;m[2][3] = 0.0;
m[3][0] = 0.0;  m[3][1] = 0.0;m[3][2] = 0.0;m[3][3] = 1.0;
}
```

3.3 Animation

This section demonstrates how dynamic motion is achieved through repetitively editing and displaying a structure network. The example is, for the most part, the same as Programming Example 3.2. We have replaced the edit session in Example 3.2 with the following code:

```
/* Set the element pointer to the label This points to
 * the label, to replace the local matrix the pointer
 * will have to be offset to the next element in the
 * structure */
psetelemptrlabel (LABEL);

/* Offset the element pointer to point to the local
 * transformation */
poffsetelemptr (1);

/* Now we are pointing to the set local transform
 * structure element in the structure network. We will
 * loop, changing the translation vector each loop to
 * move the object around the origin in a circular
 * fashion.  A translation matrix is created which
 * replaces the previous local matrix in the structure
 * network.  The structure network is re-traversed to
 * show the object in it's new position */

/* Initialize the loop toggle */
loop = 1;

/* Do for a while */
for (i=0; i<20; i++)
  {
  if (loop == 1)
    {
    /* Set translation point to origin */
    trans_vector.x = -0.5;
    trans_vector.y = -0.5;
    trans_vector.z =  0.0;
    }
  else
    {
    /* Set translation point to original position */
    trans_vector.x =  0.0;
```

```
        trans_vector.y =   0.0;
        trans_vector.z =   0.0;
        }
    /* Toggle loop counter */
    loop = -loop;

    /* Generate a 3D transformation matrix Note: this
     * DOES NOT create a structure element */
    ptranslate3 (&trans_vector, &error_ind, trans_matrix);

    /* Set the matrix as the local transformation matrix
     * Note: this creates a structure element that replaces
     * the previous element to which the element pointer is
     * pointing.  The pointer is not incremented after
     * putting this structure element into DLM (because
     * we are in replace edit mode), so the pointer will
     * still be pointing here next loop. */
    psetlocaltran3 (trans_matrix, PREPLACE);

    /* Redraw all structures posted to the workstation -
     * Because we have changed the local transformation
     * matrix in the parent structure, the child structure
     * will inherit the new transformation matrix
     * when the structure network is traversed. */
    predrawallstruct (WS_ID, PALWAYS);

    /* Sleep */
    sleep (1);

/* End do */
}
```

In the edit session of the previous example, we changed the transformation matrix and terminated the program. In the above code segment, each iteration of the for-loop changes the value of the transformation matrix. After the transformation matrix is modified, the structure is redrawn on the workstation. This *should* produce the effect of one smooth motion. Unfortunately, the motion is not always smooth, if the structure is very complex, the time that it takes to recalculate the new coordinates or to refresh the screen can be significant. If this time period is long enough the motion will be jerky or, where the time is very long, it will seem as if the image is a series of still pictures.

Another important note is that the element pointer is set to point to the translation transformation matrix once before the loop starts. When the new structure element replaces the previous transformation structure element, when edit mode is in replace, the structure element pointer is not changed. On the successive iterations of the loop, the element pointer is still pointing to the transformation structure element, which is the element we wish to replace.

Review Questions

1. What is the relationship among the global transformation, local transformation and composite transformation?

2. Using Programming Example 3.1 as a starting point, write a PHIGS program that creates a structure identified as ROOT_STRUCT. Have the root structure invoke the structure PARENT_ID and separately invoke the CHILD_ID structure.

3. What is the relationship between ROOT_STRUCT and CHILD_ID?

4. When a structure is opened, what is the value of the element pointer?

5. Using the PHIGS program written for question (2), open the root structure for editing in insert mode. Insert between the execute of the PARENT_ID structure and the CHILD_ID structure a transformation to rotate the structure 30º.

6. Using the program written in question 5, incorporate the animation loop provided in Section 3.3 in the root structure. Incorporate this same loop in the PARENT_ID structure.

4
The Wonderful World of Color

Introduction

This chapter elaborates on the use of color attributes. On completion of this chapter, the reader will be able to build color tables and create output primitives using different color models. As shown in Figure 4.1, there are three different types of color. Color representation and color approximation representation are both subtypes of indexed color. Both methods of indexed color are workstation dependent. Direct color is a *nonindexed* method of specifying color that is workstation-independent.

With PHIGS, we are able to create structures with either high-resolution TRUE color or low-resolution PSEUDO color. The resolution of the color is determined by the number of bits used to store the *color coordinate*. We shall see what is meant by color coordinate in Section 4.4. Generally, true color is 24 bits of color, that is the color coordinate is specified in 24 bits, while pseudo color is specified in 8 bits. The number of bits for each of these representations can vary, so check your individual implementation. Both true and pseudo color workstation types can be used with color representation and color approximation representation. In most instances, however, it is easier to use true color with color representation and pseudo color with color approximation representation.

When working with solid objects, parts of output primitives viewed from a perspective reference point may be obscured from view by other output primitives. These hidden parts are removed from display by hidden-line and hidden-surface removal (HLHSR). The manner in which HLHSR is performed is implementation dependent and takes precedence over display priority. When HLHSR is off, normal display priority is in effect.

HLHSR is specified for both the workstation and the structure. A structure can specify HLHSR by creating a structure element that will turn on HLHSR for the output primitives that follow in that structure. The structure is then posted to a workstation that has enabled its HLHSR mode. If either the structure HLHSR identifier or the workstation HLHSR mode has not been set, hidden lines and surfaces will not be removed. Note that structures use an HLHSR *identifier* and workstations set an HLHSR *mode*. The flexibility of the mode/identifier scheme

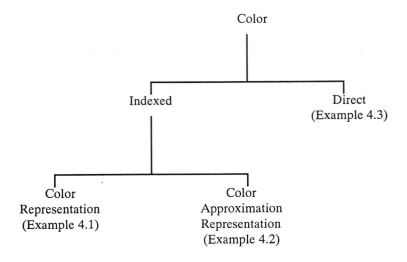

Figure 4.1. PHIGS color types.

gives the PHIGS programmer the ability to enable/disable HLHSR on a workstation-dependent basis or on a structure- or structure-element-dependent basis.

The PHIGS standard requires that the default mode for HLHSR be 0. The standard also allows the 0 mode to represent whichever HLHSR mode is most convenient to the implementation. An implementation may, therefore, use mode 0 to turn HLHSR off, while another implementation may use mode 0 to turn HLHSR on. Check your individual implementation for the proper HLHSR mode settings.

In Section 4.1 we discuss an example using color representation. In Section 4.2 we will present that same example using color approximation representation. In Section 4.3 we present this example using direct color. The three example in this chapter are visually identical when displayed on the workstation. They demonstrate a seven sided solid object, each side being a different color. Programming Example 4.1 uses indexed color, Example 4.2 uses a color approximation index, and Example 4.3 uses direct color. We have also changed the view representation to observe the object from an angle. We have included transformations and an animation sequence to rotate the object around the origin to view all sides.

Section 4.4 discusses color models. In each of these examples we use the RGB color model. The RGB color model specifies colors as percentages of red, green and blue (RGB). RGB, however, is only one of several color models used by PHIGS. In this section we compare the RGB color model with the HLS (hue, lightness, and saturation) color model.

4.1 Color Representation

As we have seen in Chapter 1, one way to specify an output primitive's color is to set a color index. Each workstation has a color table that contains a list of all the colors for that workstation. The color index specified for the output primitive is an index into this table. Since the color table for each workstation can vary, we say that the color index is workstation dependent.

Figure 4.2 graphically demonstrates how the colors can vary from workstation to workstation. The structure specifies an index of 1 into the color table for an output primitive, it then posts the structure to workstation 1 and workstation 2. The color contained in entry 1 for each of these workstations is different. The output primitive that is resultantly displayed on the workstation, therefore, is different. This can be very useful in many applications when color is a function of some characteristic of a model. If, for example, we wished to demonstrate varying stress on an object, the index into the table can be a function of the stress on the object. We can also use multiple workstations with different color tables to model different function of the same structure.

The size of the color table may vary with each implementation of PHIGS. The PHIGS standard specifies that the table must be at least two entries long. The first entry in the color epresentation table defines the workstation's

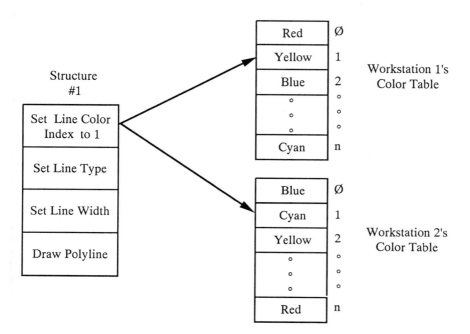

Figure 4.2. Indexed color.

background color The background color is the color of the surface after it has been cleared. The second entry in the table is the default foreground color, the drawing color.

At times, PHIGS may be limited by the underlying implementation. If the display is unable to produce the color that was specified by the graphics program, PHIGS will approximate the color. If, for example, we were to run Programming Example 4.1 on a monochrome workstation, PHIGS would produce a shade that is as close to green as possible on a monochrome workstation.

Programming Example 4.1 creates a simple structure that uses indexed color representation. This example serves as an introduction to color representation. The example customizes a color representation table, which is then used to define the color of output primitives. With this example we will show how entries within the color representation table are changed and used.

Programming Example 4.1

Programming Example 4.1 defines a view, defines color representations for the background and each of the seven sides of the object. The program then draws a reference axis and creates and animates the object. Programming Example 4.1 introduces the concept of defining color representations and simulating solid objects.

After the program opens PHIGS and a workstation, the user subroutine define_angle_view is called to establish the orientation of the viewing angle and view volume (Chapter 2). The program then calls the user subroutine define_colour_rep. The subroutine defines the background and seven foreground colors, one for each side of the object. The program then sets hidden line and hidden surface removal to simulate a solid object. The reference axis is created by the user subroutine create_axis.

When using color representation a separate color index must be set for each output primitive type to be used. The pfillarea3 output primitive will not be affected if we changed the color representation index for the polyline, text or other output primitives . In order to change the color of the interior to something other than the default foreground color we must specifically set the color for that output primitive. This is true for all output primitives when using color representation.

Note the hierarchy of the structure network. The parent structure contains the structure elements that describe the axis, a transformation, and a structure element to execute a child structure. The child structure is created by the user subroutine create_colour_fillarea. This object is a solid version of the wireframe, which was first created in Chapter 2.

Define a Colour Representation Entry

The following PHIGS function call in user subroutine define_colour_rep modifies an entry within the color representation table:

```
psetcolourrep (ws_id, 0, &table);
                        /*(PHOP,WSOP,*,*)*/
```

The function receives as input the identifier of the workstation whose table is to be modified. The second parameter to the function call specifies which entry within the color representation table is to be modified. The third parameter to the function call is the new color coordinate for the entry.

In the example we have specified a different color for each of the color indices 0 through 7. As we shall see in the following sections we will set a different interior (fill area) color index for each side of the object. Note that PHIGS uses interior and fill area synonymously. Interior is used in reference to attributes and fill area in reference to output primitives.

Set the HLHSR Mode

In order to remove hidden lines and surfaces from a workstation, the HLHSR mode must be set. The following PHIGS function call sets the HLHSR mode:

```
psethlhsrmode (WS_ID, HLHSR_ON);
                      /*(PHOP,WSOP,*,*)*/
```

The function receives as input the identifier of the workstation for which the HLHSR mode is to be set. The second parameter to the function call is the HLHSR setting. The value of this parameter is implementation-dependent, check your implementation for valid settings. In the example, a value of 1 turns on HLHSR.

Setting the HLHSR Identifier

In order to remove hidden lines and surfaces from a structure, the HLHSR identifier must be set. The following PHIGS function call creates a structure element that sets the HLHSR attribute for the structure:

```
psethlhsrid  (HLHSR_ON);
                     /*(PHOP,*,STOP,*)*/
```

The function call receives as input the HLHSR setting, which is applied to subsequent output primitives. In order for the HLHSR identifier to have an effect on the display of the structure, the HLHSR mode must be set for the workstation to which the structure is posted.

Set Interior Style

After the user subroutine create_colour_fillarea defines the vertex coordinates for the seven sides of the object, it sets the interior style to solid. The following PHIGS function call sets interior color style:

```
psetintstyle (PSOLID);         /*(PHOP,*,STOP,*)*/
```

The function receives as input an enumeration data type that describes the interior style of the polygon. The acceptable values for this function are hollow, solid, pattern, hatch, empty and general. In the example, we have set this value to solid.

Set the Interior Color Index

For each of the sides of the object, a different interior color index is used. The following PHIGS function call creates a structure element that sets the interior color index attribute:

```
psetintcolourind (1); /*(PHOP,*,STOP,*)*/
```

The function receives as input an integer value that is the index into the color representation table.

Fill Area

The fill area primitive will generate a polygon output primitive that contains a constant color. A fill area requires at least three points and may be defined as either 2- or 3-D. The pfillarea PHIGS function call creates a 2-D fill area. The following PHIGS function call creates a structure element containing the 3-D fill area output primitive:

```
pfillarea3 (5, side_1_vertex);
                          /*(PHOP,*,STOP,*)*/
```

The fillarea3 function receives as input an integer value specifying the number of vertices describing the polygon. The second input parameter is an array of type Ppoint3. This array contains the vertex coordinates for each of the verticies.

Note that the first and last vertex coordinates in the array are not coincidental. This is in contrast to the polyline3 function call that is used in Chapers 2 and 3. The polyline3 function requires that the first and last points of the array be coincidental to close the object. The pfillarea3 function call automatically connects the first and last points to enclose the interior.

After the structure is created, control returns to the main program. The structure, which posts to a workstation and drawn. We then have an animation sequence, which allows the user to view each of the sides. The operations to perform this animation have been presented in Chapter 3.

```
/*
 *                              Example 4.1
 */
#include <phigs.h>

#define WS_ID          1
#define STRUCT_ID      1
```

```
#define VIEW_ID        1
#define CHILD_ID       2
#define LABEL          1

main()
{
    Pint    i;
    Ppoint3         pt;
    Pvector3        shift;
    Pvector3        scale;
    Pfloat          angle;
    Pmatrix3        matrix;
    Pint    error;

    /* Initialize rotation setting */
    angle = 0.0;

    /* Initialize center of object,
     *        shift vector and scale */
    pt.x    = 0.0;
    pt.y    = 0.0;
    pt.z    = 0.0;
    shift.x = 0.0;
    shift.y = 0.0;
    shift.z = 0.0;
    scale.x = 1.0;
    scale.y = 1.0;
    scale.z = 1.0;

    /* Open PHIGS */
    popenphigs ("/dev/tty", 0);

    /* Open a true-color workstation */
    popenws (WS_ID, 0, PWST_OUTPUT_TRUE);

    /* Define a view for the workstation */
    define_angle_view (WS_ID, VIEW_ID);

    /* Define a table of color representations */
    define_colour_rep (WS_ID);

    /* Set HLHSR mode - This turns on z-buffering
     * for the workstation */
    psethlhsrmode (WS_ID, 1);
```

```
/* Open a parent structure */
popenstruct (STRUCT_ID);

/* Set HLHSR IDThis turns on Z-buffering for
 * this structure */
psethlhsrid (1);

/* Set the view index */
psetviewind (VIEW_ID);

/* Create an axis */
create_axis ();

/* Set a label -
 * This serves as a pointer to the following
 * structure element */
plabel (LABEL);

/* Initialize matrix to identity (normal)
 * No structure element is created, just a
 * matrix in main memory */
identity3 (matrix);

/* Set the identity matrix as the local
 * transformation matrix  A structure element is
 * created.  The label is therefore just before
 * this structure element.  Later we will come
 * back to edit this structure element
 * containing the set local transform element */
psetlocaltran3 (matrix, PREPLACE);

/* Execute the child structure The child
 * structure will be created later.  Nothing
 * will be executed until the structure
 * network is traversed (using predrawallstruct
 * or pupdatews). We cannot create child
 * structure now because we already have
 * a structure open. When executed, the child
 * structure will inherit the above
 * transformation and view from the parent. */
pexecutestruct (CHILD_ID);

/* Close the structure */
pclosestruct ();
```

```
/* Open the child structure */
popenstruct (STRUCT_ID);

/* Draw the object */
create_colour_fillarea ();

/* Close the child structure */
pclosestruct ();

/* Post the parent structure to the workstation
 * Note: only the parent structure is posted.
 * The child structure will be executed by the
 * parent. */
ppoststruct (WS_ID, STRUCT_ID, 0.0);

/* Redraw all structures posted to
 *                     the workstation */
predrawallstruct (WS_ID, PALWAYS);

/* Set edit mode to replace - This will put all
 * succeding calls into the same place in DLM so
 * that just the one set local transformation
 * instruction will be changed (Note: a common
 * mistake is to forget to reset edit mode to
 * INSERT before defining a new structure,
 * resulting in a structure which contains
 * nothing) */
pseteditmode (PEDIT_REPLACE);

/*Open parent structure so it can be edited*/
popenstruct (STRUCT_ID);

/* Set the element pointer to the beginning of
 * the parent structure - the pointer will be at
 * the end of the structure if you don't reset
 * it to the beginning */
psetelemptr (0);

/* Set the element pointer to the label - This
 * points to the  label, to replace the local
 * matrix the pointer will have to be offset to
 * the next element in the structure */
psetelemptrlabel (LABEL);
```

```
/* Offset the element pointer to point to the
 * local transformation */
poffsetelemptr (1);

/* Now we are pointing to the set local
 * transform structure  element in the structure
 * network. We'll loop, changing the translation
 * vector each loop to move the object around
 * the origin in a circular fashion. A
 * translation matrix is created which replaces
 * the previous local marix in the structure
 * network. The structure network is retraversed
 * to show the object in it's new position */

/* Do for a while */
for (i=0; i<100; i++)
  {
  /* Increment rotation values */
  angle = angle + 0.1;

  /* Build transformation matrix */
  pbuildtran3 (&pt, &shift, angle, angle, angle,
               &scale, &error, matrix);

  /* Set the local transformation matrix - This is
   * the structure element to be replaced */
   psetlocaltran3 (matrix, PPRECONCATENATE);

  /* Redraw all structures - This will redraw all
   * structures posted to the workstation */
   predrawallstruct (WS_ID, PALWAYS);

   /* Sleep */
   sleep (1);
  }
/* End do */

/* Close the structure that was open for editing
 * This is often forgotten, creating a state
 * error when trying to open another structure*/
pclosestruct ();

/* Set edit mode to insert - Although this it
 * not necessary in this example (as no more
 * structure creation will take place), it is a
```

```
       * good idea to get into the habit of always re-
       * setting the edit mode to insert (the
       * default).  Forgetting to do so will cause
       * problems later in more complex programs.
       * You will be in a situation where every
       * structure element is overwritten, creating
       * structures containing nothing */
      pseteditmode (PEDIT_INSERT);

      /* Close the workstation */
      pclosews (WS_ID);

      /* Close PHIGS */
      pclosephigs ();
}


create_colour_fillarea ()
{
#include <phigs.h>

    Ppoint3   side_1_vertex[5];
    Ppoint3   side_2_vertex[4];
    Ppoint3   side_3_vertex[5];
    Ppoint3   side_4_vertex[4];
    Ppoint3   side_5_vertex[4];
    Ppoint3   side_6_vertex[4];
    Ppoint3   side_7_vertex[4];

    /* Initialize side 1 vertices */
     side_1_vertex[0].x = -0.1;
     side_1_vertex[0].y = -0.1;
     side_1_vertex[0].z =  0.1;
     side_1_vertex[1].x =  0.1;
     side_1_vertex[1].y = -0.1;
     side_1_vertex[1].z =  0.1;
     side_1_vertex[2].x =  0.1;
     side_1_vertex[2].y =  0.0;
     side_1_vertex[2].z =  0.1;
     side_1_vertex[3].x =  0.0;
     side_1_vertex[3].y =  0.1;
     side_1_vertex[3].z =  0.1;
     side_1_vertex[4].x = -0.1;
     side_1_vertex[4].y =  0.1;
     side_1_vertex[4].z =  0.1;
```

```
/* Initialize side 2 vertices */
 side_2_vertex[0].x =  0.1;
 side_2_vertex[0].y = -0.1;
 side_2_vertex[0].z =  0.1;
 side_2_vertex[1].x =  0.1;
 side_2_vertex[1].y = -0.1;
 side_2_vertex[1].z = -0.1;
 side_2_vertex[2].x =  0.1;
 side_2_vertex[2].y =  0.0;
 side_2_vertex[2].z = -0.1;
 side_2_vertex[3].x =  0.1;
 side_2_vertex[3].y =  0.0;
 side_2_vertex[3].z =  0.1;

/* Initialize side 3 vertices */
 side_3_vertex[0].x = -0.1;
 side_3_vertex[0].y = -0.1;
 side_3_vertex[0].z = -0.1;
 side_3_vertex[1].x =  0.1;
 side_3_vertex[1].y = -0.1;
 side_3_vertex[1].z = -0.1;
 side_3_vertex[2].x =  0.1;
 side_3_vertex[2].y =  0.0;
 side_3_vertex[2].z = -0.1;
 side_3_vertex[3].x =  0.0;
 side_3_vertex[3].y =  0.1;
 side_3_vertex[3].z = -0.1;
 side_3_vertex[4].x = -0.1;
 side_3_vertex[4].y =  0.1;
 side_3_vertex[4].z = -0.1;

/* Initialize side 4 vertices */
 side_4_vertex[0].x = -0.1;
 side_4_vertex[0].y = -0.1;
 side_4_vertex[0].z = -0.1;
 side_4_vertex[1].x = -0.1;
 side_4_vertex[1].y = -0.1;
 side_4_vertex[1].z =  0.1;
 side_4_vertex[2].x = -0.1;
 side_4_vertex[2].y =  0.1;
 side_4_vertex[2].z =  0.1;
 side_4_vertex[3].x = -0.1;
 side_4_vertex[3].y =  0.1;
 side_4_vertex[3].z = -0.1;
```

```
/* Initialize side 5 vertices */
 side_5_vertex[0].x = -0.1;
 side_5_vertex[0].y =  0.1;
 side_5_vertex[0].z =  0.1;
 side_5_vertex[1].x =  0.0;
 side_5_vertex[1].y =  0.1;
 side_5_vertex[1].z =  0.1;
 side_5_vertex[2].x =  0.0;
 side_5_vertex[2].y =  0.1;
 side_5_vertex[2].z = -0.1;
 side_5_vertex[3].x = -0.1;
 side_5_vertex[3].y =  0.1;
 side_5_vertex[3].z = -0.1;

/* Initialize side 6 vertices */
 side_6_vertex[0].x = -0.1;
 side_6_vertex[0].y = -0.1;
 side_6_vertex[0].z =  0.1;
 side_6_vertex[1].x =  0.1;
 side_6_vertex[1].y = -0.1;
 side_6_vertex[1].z =  0.1;
 side_6_vertex[2].x =  0.1;
 side_6_vertex[2].y = -0.1;
 side_6_vertex[2].z = -0.1;
 side_6_vertex[3].x = -0.1;
 side_6_vertex[3].y = -0.1;
 side_6_vertex[3].z = -0.1;

/* Initialize side 7 vertices */
 side_7_vertex[0].x =  0.0;
 side_7_vertex[0].y =  0.1;
 side_7_vertex[0].z =  0.1;
 side_7_vertex[1].x =  0.1;
 side_7_vertex[1].y =  0.0;
 side_7_vertex[1].z =  0.1;
 side_7_vertex[2].x =  0.1;
 side_7_vertex[2].y =  0.0;
 side_7_vertex[2].z = -0.1;
 side_7_vertex[3].x =  0.0;
 side_7_vertex[3].y =  0.1;
 side_7_vertex[3].z = -0.1;

/* Set the interior style to solid */
psetintstyle (PSOLID);
```

```
    /* Set the color and create a fillarea primitive
     * structure element for each side */
    psetintcolourind (1);
    pfillarea3 (5, side_1_vertex);

    psetintcolourind (2);
    pfillarea3 (4, side_2_vertex);

    psetintcolourind (3);
    pfillarea3 (5, side_3_vertex);

    psetintcolourind (4);
    pfillarea3 (4, side_4_vertex);

    psetintcolourind (5);
    pfillarea3 (4, side_5_vertex);

    psetintcolourind (6);
    pfillarea3 (4, side_6_vertex);

    psetintcolourind (7);
    pfillarea3 (4, side_7_vertex);
}




define_angle_view(ws_id, view_index)
int ws_id, view_index;
{
#include <phigs.h>

    static Ppoint3f    vrp        = { 0.0, 0.0, 0.0};
    static Ppoint3f    vpn        = { 0.7, 0.7, 0.7};
    static Ppoint3f    vup        = { 0.0, 1.0, 0.0};
    static Ppoint3f    prp        = { 0.0, 0.0, 2.0};
    static Plimit      window
                            = {-0.5, 0.5,-0.5, 0.5};
    static Plimit3     viewport
                = { 0.0, 1.0, 0.0, 1.0, 0.0, 1.0};
```

```
static Pfloat          back       =  -1.0;
static Pfloat          view       =   0.0;
static Pfloat          front      =   1.0;
Pviewrep3              rep;
Pviewmapping3          mapping;
Pint                   err;

/* Calculate view orientation matrix for
 * SET VIEW REPRESENTATION */
pevalvieworientationmatrix3
  (&vrp, &vpn, &vup, &err,
                    rep.orientation_matrix);

/* Define view mapping data */
mapping.window       = window;
mapping.viewport     = viewport;
mapping.proj         = PPERSPECTIVE;
mapping.prp          = prp;
mapping.view_plane   = view;
mapping.back_plane   = back;
mapping.front_plane  = front;

/* Generate 3-D transform matrix to project VRC
 * window to NPC viewport */
pevalviewmappingmatrix3
        (&mapping, &err, rep.mapping_matrix);

/*Define boundaries of area in
 *  NPC space which can be displayed */
rep.clip_limit.xmin =  0.0;
rep.clip_limit.ymin =  0.0;
rep.clip_limit.zmin =  0.0;
rep.clip_limit.xmax =  1.0;
rep.clip_limit.ymax =  1.0;
rep.clip_limit.zmax =  1.0;

/* Disable X, Y and Z clipping */
rep.clip_xy          = PNOCLIP;
rep.clip_back        = PNOCLIP;
rep.clip_front       = PNOCLIP;
/* Define 3-D view representation entry on
 *       workstation view table */
psetviewrep3 (ws_id, view_index, &rep);
}
```

```
define_colour_rep (ws_id)
int    ws_id;
{
#include <phigs.h>

  Pcobundl  table[1];

    /* Assign red, green and blue values  -
     * equal parts (will yield white)
     * table[*].x = RED;
     * table[*].y = GREEN; table[*].z = BLUE       */
    table[0].x = 0.0;
    table[0].y = 0.0;
    table[0].z = 0.0;

    /* Set color representation for index 0 */
    psetcolourrep (ws_id, 0, &table);

    /* Assign red, green and blue values */
    table[0].x = 1.0;
    table[0].y = 0.0;
    table[0].z = 0.0;

    /* Set color representation for index 1 */
    psetcolourrep (ws_id, 1, &table);

    /* Assign red, green and blue values */
    table[0].x = 0.0;
    table[0].y = 1.0;
    table[0].z = 0.0;

    /* Set color representation for index 2 */
    psetcolourrep (ws_id, 2, &table);

    /* Assign red, green and blue values */
    table[0].x = 0.0;
    table[0].y = 0.0;
    table[0].z = 1.0;

    /* Set color representation for index 3 */
    psetcolourrep (ws_id, 3, &table);

    /* Assign red, green and blue values */
    table[0].x = 1.0;
```

```
table[0].y = 1.0;
table[0].z = 0.0;

/* Set color representation for index 4 */
psetcolourrep (ws_id, 4, &table);

/* Assign red, green and blue values */
table[0].x = 1.0;
table[0].y = 0.0;
table[0].z = 1.0;

/* Set color representation for index 5 */
psetcolourrep (ws_id, 5, &table);

/* Assign red, green and blue values */
table[0].x = 0.0;
table[0].y = 1.0;
table[0].z = 1.0;

/* Set color representation for index 6 */
psetcolourrep (ws_id, 6, &table);

/* Assign red, green and blue values */
table[0].x = 0.8;
table[0].y = 0.5;
table[0].z = 0.2;

/* Set color representation for index 7 */
psetcolourrep (ws_id, 7, &table);
}
```

4.2 Color Approximation Representation

As we shall see in the folllowing example, color approximation representation is similar to color representation. As stated in the previous section, each workstation has an associated color representation table. Just as we set an index for an output primitive on a true color workstation, we shall also set an index for output primitives for pseudo-color workstations.

The main difference between color representation and color approximation representation is the resolution of the colors. With color representation we are given 24 bits to describe a color, with color approximation we are only provided 8 bits of color. Although the specific number of bits may vary with your implementation, the number of bits for true-color representation is significantly greater than the number of bits provided for pseudo-color.

When using color representation we define a color index for each type of the output primitive. This is not the case with color approximation representation. Once a color approximation index has been specified for the structure, all output primitives are drawn in that color until the color approximation index is changed.

Programming Example 4.2

Programming Example 4.2 defines a view and color approximation representations for the background and each of the seven sides of the object. The program then draws a reference axis and creates and animates the object. Programming Example 4.2 introduces the concept of defining color approximation representations. The only difference between Examples 4.2 and 4.1 is the use of color approximation representation rather than color representation.

After the program opens PHIGS and a pseudo-color workstation, the user subroutine define_angle_view is called to establish the orientation of the viewing angle and view volume (Chapter 2). The program then calls the user subroutine define_approx_rep. The subroutine defines the background and seven foreground colors, one for each side of the object. The program then sets hidden-line and hidden-surface removal to simulate a solid object. The reference axis is created by the user subroutine create_axis. Prior to the creation of this axis, we set the color approximation index.

The object is created by the user subroutine create_approx_fillarea. The only difference between this and the create_colour_fillarea subroutine is the use of the PHIGS function call psetcolourapproxind in place of psetintcolourind. When using color approximation there is a single-color approximation index for all output primitives. This is contrasted to using color representation that has a separate color index for each output primitive type.

Set Color Approximation Index

For each of the sides of the object, a different color approximation index is used. The following PHIGS function call creates a structure element that sets the color approximation index attribute:

```
psetcolourapproxind (3);      /*(PHOP,*,STOP,*)*/
```

The function receives as input an integer value, which is the index into the color approximation representation table.

Define a Color Representation Entry

The following PHIGS function call in user subroutine define_aprox_rep modifies an entry within the color approximation representation table:

```
psetcolouraproxrep (ws_id, 0, &table);
                              /*(PHOP,WSOP,*,*)*/
```

The function receives as input the identifier of the workstation whose table is to be modified. The second parameter to the function call specifies which entry within the color approximation representation table is to be modified. The third parameter to the function call is the new color coordinate for the entry.

In the example we have specified a different color for each of the color inidices 0 through 7. As we shall see in the following sections, we will set a different interior (fill area) color index for each side of the object.

```
/*
 *                              Example 4.2
 */
#include <phigs.h>

#define       WS_ID        1
#define       STRUCT_ID    1
#define VIEW_ID            1
#define CHILD_ID           2
#define LABEL              1

main()
{
    Pint     i;
    Ppoint3        pt;
    Pvector3       shift;
    Pvector3       scale;
    Pfloat         angle;
    Pmatrix3       matrix;
    Pint     error;

    /* Initialize rotation setting */
    angle = 0.0;

    /* Initialize center of object, shift vector
     * and scale */
    pt.x    = 0.0;
    pt.y    = 0.0;
    pt.z    = 0.0;
    shift.x = 0.0;
    shift.y = 0.0;
    shift.z = 0.0;
    scale.x = 1.0;
    scale.y = 1.0;
    scale.z = 1.0;
```

```
/* Open PHIGS */
popenphigs ("/dev/tty", 0);

/* open a pseudo-color workstation */
popenws (WS_ID, 0, PWST_OUTPUT_PSEUDO);

/* Define a view for the workstation */
define_angle_view (WS_ID, VIEW_ID);

/* Define a table of color approximations */
define_approx_rep (WS_ID);

/* Set HLHSR mode
 * This turns on z-buffering for the
 * workstation */
psethlhsrmode (WS_ID, 1);

/* Open a parent structure */
popenstruct (STRUCT_ID);

/* Set HLHSR ID
 * This turns on Z-buffering for
 *                         this structure */
psethlhsrid (1);

/* Set the view index */
psetviewind (VIEW_ID);

/* Set axis color -
 * Polyline color representation index is set in
 * the axis routine. We must set the color
 * approximation index here */
psetcolourapproxind (2);

/* Create an axis */
create_axis ();

/* Set a label - This serves as a pointer to the
 * following structure element */
plabel (LABEL);

/* Initialize matrix to identity (normal) - No
 * structure element is created, just a matrix
 * in main memory */
identity3 (matrix);
```

```
/* Set the identity matrix as the local
 * transformation matrix  A structure element is
 * created.  The label is therefore just
 * before this structure element.  Later we will
 * come back to edit this structure element
 * containing the set local transform element */
psetlocaltran3 (matrix, PREPLACE);

/* Execute the child structure - The child
 * structure will be created later. Nothing will
 * be executed until the structure network is
 * traversed (using predrawallstruct or
 * pupdatews). We cannot create child structure
 * now because we already have a structure open.
 * When executed, the child structure will
 * inherit the above transformation and view
 * from the parent. */
pexecutestruct (CHILD_ID);

/* Close the structure */
pclosestruct ();

/* Open the child structure */
popenstruct (STRUCT_ID);

/* Draw the object */
create_approx_fillarea ();

/* Close the child structure */
pclosestruct ();

/* Post the parent structure to the workstation
 * Note: only the parent structure is posted.
 * The child structure will be executed by the
 * parent. */
ppoststruct (WS_ID, STRUCT_ID, 0.0);

/*Redraw all structures posted to
 *                        the workstation */
predrawallstruct (WS_ID, PALWAYS);

/* Set edit mode to replace - This will put all
 * succeeding  calls into the same place in DLM
 * so that just the one set  local
 * transformation instruction will be changed
```

```
 * (Note: a common mistake is to forget to reset
 * edit mode to INSERT  before defining a new
 * structure, resulting in a structure
 * which contains nothing) */
pseteditmode (PEDIT_REPLACE);

/*Open parent structure so it can be edited */
popenstruct (STRUCT_ID);

/* Set the element pointer to the beginning of
 * the parent structure - the pointer will be at
 * the end of the structure if you don't reset
 * it to the beginning */
psetelemptr (0);

/* Set the element pointer to the label - This
 * points to the  label, to replace the local
 * matrix the pointer will have to  be offset to
 * the next element in the structure */
psetelemptrlabel (LABEL);

/* Offset the element pointer to point to
 * the local transformation */
poffsetelemptr (1);

/* Now we are pointing to the set local
 * transform structure element in the structure
 * network. We'll loop, changing  the
 * translation vector each loop to move the
 * object around  the origin in a circular
 * fashion.  A translation matrix is  created
 * which replaces the previous local marix
 * in the  structure network.  The structure
 * network is re-traversed to show the object in
 * it's new position */

/* Do for a while */
for (i=0; i<100; i++)
  {
  /* Increment rotation values */
  angle = angle + 0.1;
```

```
/* Build transformation matrix */
    pbuildtran3 (&pt, &shift, angle, angle, angle,
                &scale, &error, matrix);
/* Set the local transformation matrix - This is
 * the structure element to be replaced */
    psetlocaltran3 (matrix, PPRECONCATENATE);

/* Redraw all structures - This will redraw all
 * structures posted to the workstation */
    predrawallstruct (WS_ID, PALWAYS);

        /* Sleep */
        sleep (1);
}
/* End do */

/* Close the structure that was open for editing
 * This is often forgotten, creating a state
 * error when trying to open another structure*/
pclosestruct ();

/* Set edit mode to insert - Although this is
 * not necessary in  this example (as no more
 * structure creation will take place),
 * it is a good idea to get into the habit of
 * always re-setting  the edit mode to insert
 * (the default).  Forgetting to do so will
 * cause problems later in more complex
 * programs.  You will be in a situation where
 * every structure element is  overwritten,
 * creating structures containing nothing */
pseteditmode (PEDIT_INSERT);

/* Close the workstation */
pclosews (WS_ID);

/* Close PHIGS */
pclosephigs ();
}
```

```
create_approx_fillarea ()
{
#include <phigs.h>

    Ppoint3    side_1_vertex[5];
    Ppoint3    side_2_vertex[4];
    Ppoint3    side_3_vertex[5];
    Ppoint3    side_4_vertex[4];
    Ppoint3    side_5_vertex[4];
    Ppoint3    side_6_vertex[4];
    Ppoint3    side_7_vertex[4];

    /* Initialize side 1 vertices */
     side_1_vertex[0].x = -0.1;
     side_1_vertex[0].y = -0.1;
     side_1_vertex[0].z =  0.1;
     side_1_vertex[1].x =  0.1;
     side_1_vertex[1].y = -0.1;
     side_1_vertex[1].z =  0.1;
     side_1_vertex[2].x =  0.1;
     side_1_vertex[2].y =  0.0;
     side_1_vertex[2].z =  0.1;
     side_1_vertex[3].x =  0.0;
     side_1_vertex[3].y =  0.1;
     side_1_vertex[3].z =  0.1;
     side_1_vertex[4].x = -0.1;
     side_1_vertex[4].y =  0.1;
     side_1_vertex[4].z =  0.1;

    /* Initialize side 2 vertices */
     side_2_vertex[0].x =  0.1;
     side_2_vertex[0].y = -0.1;
     side_2_vertex[0].z =  0.1;
     side_2_vertex[1].x =  0.1;
     side_2_vertex[1].y = -0.1;
     side_2_vertex[1].z = -0.1;
     side_2_vertex[2].x =  0.1;
     side_2_vertex[2].y =  0.0;
     side_2_vertex[2].z = -0.1;
     side_2_vertex[3].x =  0.1;
     side_2_vertex[3].y =  0.0;
     side_2_vertex[3].z =  0.1;
```

```
/* Initialize side 3 vertices */
 side_3_vertex[0].x = -0.1;
 side_3_vertex[0].y = -0.1;
 side_3_vertex[0].z = -0.1;
 side_3_vertex[1].x =  0.1;
 side_3_vertex[1].y = -0.1;
 side_3_vertex[1].z = -0.1;
 side_3_vertex[2].x =  0.1;
 side_3_vertex[2].y =  0.0;
 side_3_vertex[2].z = -0.1;
 side_3_vertex[3].x =  0.0;
 side_3_vertex[3].y =  0.1;
 side_3_vertex[3].z = -0.1;
 side_3_vertex[4].x = -0.1;
 side_3_vertex[4].y =  0.1;
 side_3_vertex[4].z = -0.1;

/* Initialize side 4 vertices */
 side_4_vertex[0].x = -0.1;
 side_4_vertex[0].y = -0.1;
 side_4_vertex[0].z = -0.1;
 side_4_vertex[1].x = -0.1;
 side_4_vertex[1].y = -0.1;
 side_4_vertex[1].z =  0.1;
 side_4_vertex[2].x = -0.1;
 side_4_vertex[2].y =  0.1;
 side_4_vertex[2].z =  0.1;
 side_4_vertex[3].x = -0.1;
 side_4_vertex[3].y =  0.1;
 side_4_vertex[3].z = -0.1;

/* Initialize side 5 vertices */
 side_5_vertex[0].x = -0.1;
 side_5_vertex[0].y =  0.1;
 side_5_vertex[0].z =  0.1;
 side_5_vertex[1].x =  0.0;
 side_5_vertex[1].y =  0.1;
 side_5_vertex[1].z =  0.1;
 side_5_vertex[2].x =  0.0;
 side_5_vertex[2].y =  0.1;
 side_5_vertex[2].z = -0.1;
 side_5_vertex[3].x = -0.1;
 side_5_vertex[3].y =  0.1;
 side_5_vertex[3].z = -0.1;
```

```
/* Initialize side 6 vertices */
 side_6_vertex[0].x = -0.1;
 side_6_vertex[0].y = -0.1;
 side_6_vertex[0].z =  0.1;
 side_6_vertex[1].x =  0.1;
 side_6_vertex[1].y = -0.1;
 side_6_vertex[1].z =  0.1;
 side_6_vertex[2].x =  0.1;
 side_6_vertex[2].y = -0.1;
 side_6_vertex[2].z = -0.1;
 side_6_vertex[3].x = -0.1;
 side_6_vertex[3].y = -0.1;
 side_6_vertex[3].z = -0.1;

/* Initialize side 7 vertices */
 side_7_vertex[0].x =  0.0;
 side_7_vertex[0].y =  0.1;
 side_7_vertex[0].z =  0.1;
 side_7_vertex[1].x =  0.1;
 side_7_vertex[1].y =  0.0;
 side_7_vertex[1].z =  0.1;
 side_7_vertex[2].x =  0.1;
 side_7_vertex[2].y =  0.0;
 side_7_vertex[2].z = -0.1;
 side_7_vertex[3].x =  0.0;
 side_7_vertex[3].y =  0.1;
 side_7_vertex[3].z = -0.1;

/* Set the interior style to solid */
psetintstyle (PSOLID);

/* Set the color and create a fillarea
 * primitive structure element  for each side */
psetcolourapproxind (1);
pfillarea3 (5, side_1_vertex);

psetcolourapproxind (2);
pfillarea3 (4, side_2_vertex);

psetcolourapproxind (3);
pfillarea3 (5, side_3_vertex);

psetcolourapproxind (4);
pfillarea3 (4, side_4_vertex);
```

```
    psetcolourapproxind (5);
    pfillarea3 (4, side_5_vertex);

    psetcolourapproxind (6);
    pfillarea3 (4, side_6_vertex);

    psetcolourapproxind (7);
    pfillarea3 (4, side_7_vertex);
}



define_approx_rep(ws_id)
int    ws_id;
{
#include <phigs.h>

    Pcoapproxbundl rep;
    Pcobundl table [1];

    /* Assign constants to color approx
     * representation data structure */
    rep.method     = PPSEUDO;
                    /* psuedo (8-bit) color */
    rep.record.pseudo.range = 1;
                    /* # entries in table    */
    rep.record.pseudo.weight[0] = 0.33;
                    /*     We'll give RGB    */
    rep.record.pseudo.weight[1] = 0.33;
                    /*       equal weight    */
    rep.record.pseudo.weight[2] = 0.33;
                    /*        for now.       */
    rep.record.pseudo.model = PCM_RGB;
                    /*        use RGB        */

    /* Assign red, green and blue values to the
     * background color. 0 is the background and 1
     * the foreground by default */
    table[0].x = 0.0;
    table[0].y = 0.0;
    table[0].z = 0.0;

    /* Assign RGB values to color approx
     * representation data  structure */
    rep.record.pseudo.colours = table;
```

```
/* Set color approximation representation
 * for index 0 */
psetcolourapproxrep (ws_id, 0, &rep);

/* Assign red, green and blue values */
table[0].x = 1.0;
table[0].y = 0.0;
table[0].z = 0.0;

/* Assign RGB values to color approx
 * representation data structure */
rep.record.pseudo.colours = table;

/* Set color approximation representation
 *                         for index 1 */
psetcolourapproxrep (ws_id, 1, &rep);

/* Assign red, green and blue values */
table[0].x = 0.0;
table[0].y = 1.0;
table[0].z = 0.0;

/* Assign RGB values to color approx
 * representation data  structure */
rep.record.pseudo.colours = table;

/* Set color approximation representation
 *                         for index 2 */
psetcolourapproxrep (ws_id, 2, &rep);

/* Assign red, green and blue values */
table[0].x = 0.0;
table[0].y = 0.0;
table[0].z = 1.0;

/* Assign RGB values to color approx
 * representation data structure */
rep.record.pseudo.colours = table;

/* Set color approximation representation
 *                         for index 3 */
psetcolourapproxrep (ws_id, 3, &rep);
```

```
/* Assign red, green and blue values */
table[0].x = 1.0;
table[0].y = 1.0;
table[0].z = 0.0;

/* Assign RGB values to color approx
 * representation data structure */
rep.record.pseudo.colours = table;

/* Set color approximation representation
 * for index 4 */
psetcolourapproxrep (ws_id, 4, &rep);

/* Assign red, green and blue values */
table[0].x = 1.0;
table[0].y = 0.0;
table[0].z = 1.0;

/* Assign RGB values to color approx
 * representation data structure */
rep.record.pseudo.colours = table;

/* Set color approximation representation for
 * index 5 */
psetcolourapproxrep (ws_id, 5, &rep);

/* Assign red, green and blue values */
table[0].x = 0.0;
table[0].y = 1.0;
table[0].z = 1.0;

/* Assign RGB values to color approx
 * representation data  structure */
rep.record.pseudo.colours = table;

/* Set color approximation representation for
 * index 6 */
psetcolourapproxrep (ws_id, 6, &rep);

/* Assign red, green and blue values */
table[0].x = 0.8;
table[0].y = 0.5;
table[0].z = 0.2;
```

```
/* Assign RGB values to color approx
 * representation data structure */
rep.record.pseudo.colours = table;

/* Set color approximation representation for
 * index 7 */
psetcolourapproxrep (ws_id, 7, &rep);
}
```

4.3 Direct Color

Direct color is a third alternative to color selection. Direct color provides the graphics program with a significantly larger palette of colors that are independent of the workstation's color tables. Direct color can also be performed in each of the color models that are supported by PHIGS.

The size of the palette, when using index color, is limited by the size of the color table. The PHIGS standard requires only that these tables are of a size to accommodate two elements. Resultantly, the palette on some implementations may not be large enough to facilitate the effects desired by the PHIGS program. Direct color specifies the actual color coordinate that is to be used by PHIGS for the output primitive as a structure element. *STOP AND THINK ABOUT THIS.* The PHIGS program is freed from using a specific number of colors and is given access to any color that is accessible in the color model.

In the two previous sections, we learned that each workstation is associated with a color table. As structures are created, output primitives access the colors on these tables via indices. If the colors for an index vary between workstations, so too does the color of the output primitive that is using that entry. If a workstation changes its color table, all output primitives using indexed color from that table change in color. In many instances, this may be desirable, while in others, a specific color for an output primitive may be desired that is independent of the workstation's color table. Since direct color uses a coordinate of a color model and not a reference to a workstation color table, output primitives displayed with direct color will not change when a color is modified in a color table.

In order to use direct color we must tell PHIGS which output primitives are to be direct. The source of the color, whether it be direct or indexed, is based on the setting of the color source flag (CSF). Prior to using direct color the CSF must be set to direct. The default setting of the CSF may vary on some implementations. As we shall see in the programming example, each output primitive type has a CSF. Polyline output primitives, therefore, may be drawn with direct color while text output primitives may be drawn to same workstation with indexed color. It is advised that check the default CSF of your implementation. Programming Example 4.3 demonstrates setting the CSF and using direct color with the RGB color model.

Programming Example 4.3

Programming Example 4.3 defines a view, sets the CSF, draws a reference axis and creates and animates the object. Programming Example 4.3 introduces the concepts of the CSF and direct color.

After the program opens PHIGS and a true-color workstation, the user subroutine define_angle_view is called to establish the orientation of the viewing angle and view volume (Chapter 2). The program then sets hidden-line and hidden-surface removal to simulate a solid object. The reference axis is created by the user subroutine create_axis.

Setting the Color Source Flag

The source, indexed or direct, of the output primitives color attribute is determined by the attribute's CSF. The following PHIGS function creates a structure element that sets the CSF of the specified output primitive:

```
psetindivcsf (PPOLYLINE, PDIRECT);
                      /*(PHOP,*,STOP,*) */
```

The function receives as input the output primitive identifier and the color source. The output primitive identifier is an enumeration type that identifies which output primitive's CSF is to be set. The following are the elements of the enumeration type: PPOLYLINE, PPOLYMARKER, PTEXT, PINTERIOR, PEDGE.

The color source is either direct or indexed. The color source attribute of the output primitive identified by the first parameter is set to the color source identified by the second parameter.

In the example program, we have set the attribute of the interior to be direct. All subsequent fill area color attributes are set to direct until the program specifically resets the CSF to indexed or until control returns to the parent structure. Remember that the parent does not inherit the attributes of the child. The CSF in a parent structure will, therefore, remain unchanged if reset by a child structure. *STOP AND THINK ABOUT THIS.* The color attributes of other output primitives are not affected by this function call and retain the original default value. If there are other output primitives whose CSF's are to be set to direct, they must be individually set.

Specifying a Direct Color

The following PHIGS function sets the color for the polyline output primitive:

```
psetintcolour (PCM_RGB, colour);
                      /*(PHOP,*,STOP*)*/
```

The function receives as input the color model that is to be used for the output primitive and a color coordinate that specifies the color of the output primitive in a Pcolor data structure named "color."

If a color coordinate other than the default is to be used for an output primitive type, it must be specifically set with a similar call. For example, the PHIGS function psettextcolor sets the direct color of the text output primitive. Each of these calls works in the same way. They receive as input the color model and color coordinate. They create, in the open structure, a structure element that sets the color of all subsequent output primitives of that type. The following functions set the direct color attributes for each of the output primitives:

> Set polyline color;
> Set marker color;
> Set text color;
> Set interior color.

The example program continues to fill the structure with fill areas of varying colors. The subroutine returns control to the calling program where the structure is posted to a workstation and animated.

```
/*
 *                              Example 4.3
 */
#include <phigs.h>

#define     WS_ID        1
#define     STRUCT_ID    1
#define     VIEW_ID      1
#define     CHILD_ID     2
#define     LABEL        1

main()
{
    Pint    i;
    Ppoint3        pt;
    Pvector3       shift;
    Pvector3       scale;
    Pfloat         angle;
    Pmatrix3       matrix;
    Pint    error;

    /* Initialize rotation setting */
    angle = 0.0;

    /* Initialize center of object, shift vector
     *                              and scale */
```

```
pt.x    = 0.0;
pt.y    = 0.0;
pt.z    = 0.0;
shift.x = 0.0;
shift.y = 0.0;
shift.z = 0.0;
scale.x = 1.0;
scale.y = 1.0;
scale.z = 1.0;

/* Open PHIGS */
popenphigs ("/dev/tty", 0);

/* Open a true-color workstation */
popenws (WS_ID, 0, PWST_OUTPUT_TRUE);

/* Define a view for the workstation */
define_angle_view (WS_ID, VIEW_ID);

/* Set HLHSR mode  This turns on z-buffering for
 *                            the workstation */
psethlhsrmode (WS_ID, 1);

/* Open a parent structure */
popenstruct (STRUCT_ID);

/* Set HLHSR ID  This turns on Z-buffering for
 *                            This structure */
psethlhsrid (1);

/* Set the view index */
psetviewind (VIEW_ID);

/* Create an axis */
create_axis ();

/* Set a label This serves as a pointer to the
 * following structure element */
plabel (LABEL);

/* Initialize matrix to identity (normal) No
 * structure element is created, just a matrix
 * in main memory */
identity3 (matrix);
```

```
/* Set the identity matrix as the local
 * transformation matrix  A structure element is
 * created.  The label is therefore just before
 * this structure element.  Later we will come
 * back to edit this structure element
 * containing the set local transform element */
psetlocaltran3 (matrix, PREPLACE);

/* Execute the child structure -
 * The child structure will be created later.
 * Nothing will be executed until the structure
 * network is raversed (using redrawallstruct or
 * pupdatews).  We cannot create child structure
 * now because we already have a structure open.
 * When executed, the child structure will
 * inherit the above transformation and view
 * from the parent. */
pexecutestruct (CHILD_ID);

/* Close the structure */
pclosestruct ();

/* Open the child structure */
popenstruct (STRUCT_ID);

/* Set the individual color source flag - This
 * allows us to use direct color */
psetindivcsf (1, PDIRECT);

/* Draw the object */
create_direct_fillarea ();

/* Close the child structure */
pclosestruct ();

/* Post the parent structure to the workstation
 * Note: only the parent structure is posted.
 * The child structure will be executed by the
 * parent. */
ppoststruct (WS_ID, STRUCT_ID, 0.0);

/* Redraw all structures posted to the
 * workstation */
predrawallstruct (WS_ID, PALWAYS);
```

```
/* Set edit mode to replace - This will put all
 * succeding calls into the same place in DLM so
 * that just the one set local  transformation
 * instruction will be changed (Note: a common
 * mistake is to forget to reset edit mode to
 * INSERT before defining a new structure,
 * resulting in a structure which  contains
 * nothing) */
pseteditmode (PEDIT_REPLACE);

/*Open the parent structure so it can
 *                          be edited*/
popenstruct (STRUCT_ID);

/* Set the element pointer to the beginning of
 * the parent structure - the pointer will be at
 * the end of the structure  if you don't reset
 * it to the beginning */
psetelemptr (0);

/* Set the element pointer to the label - This
 * points to the label, to replace the local
 * matrix the pointer will have to be offset to
 * the next element in the structure */
psetelemptrlabel (LABEL);

/* Offset the element pointer to point to the
 * local transformation */
poffsetelemptr (1);

/* Now we are pointing to the set local
 * transform structure element in the structure
 * network.  We'll loop, changing the
 * translation vector each loop to move the
 * object around the  origin in a circular
 * fashion.  A translation matrix is  created
 * which replaces the previous local marix in
 * the structure network.  The structure network
 * is re-traversed to  show the object in it's
 * new position */

/* Do for a while */
for (i=0; i<100; i++)
```

```
    {
    /* Increment rotation values */
    angle = angle + 0.1;

    /* Build transformation matrix */
    pbuildtran3 (&pt, &shift, angle, angle, angle,
                 &scale, &error, matrix);

    /* Set the local transformation matrix - This is
     * the structure element to be replaced */
     psetlocaltran3 (matrix, PPRECONCATENATE);

    /* Redraw all structures - This will redraw all
     * structures osted to the workstation */
     predrawallstruct (WS_ID, PALWAYS);

      /* Sleep */
      sleep (1);
    }
/* End do */

/* Close the structure that was open for editing
 * This is often forgotten, creating a state
 * error when trying to open another
 * structure */
pclosestruct ();

/* Set edit mode to insert - Although this it
 * not necessary in this example (as no more
 * structure creation will take place), it is a
 * good idea to get into the habit of always
 * resetting the edit mode to insert (the
 * default).  Forgetting to do so will cause
 * problems later in more complex programs.  You
 * will  be in a situation where every structure
 * element is overwritten, creating structures
 * containing nothing */
pseteditmode (PEDIT_INSERT);

/* Close the workstation */
pclosews (WS_ID);

/* Close PHIGS */
pclosephigs ();
}
```

```
create_direct_fillarea ()
{
#include <phigs.h>

    Ppoint3   side_1_vertex[5];
    Ppoint3   side_2_vertex[4];
    Ppoint3   side_3_vertex[5];
    Ppoint3   side_4_vertex[4];
    Ppoint3   side_5_vertex[4];
    Ppoint3   side_6_vertex[4];
    Ppoint3   side_7_vertex[4];

    Pcolour   colour;

    /* Initialize side 1 vertices */
     side_1_vertex[0].x = -0.1;
     side_1_vertex[0].y = -0.1;
     side_1_vertex[0].z =  0.1;
     side_1_vertex[1].x =  0.1;
     side_1_vertex[1].y = -0.1;
     side_1_vertex[1].z =  0.1;
     side_1_vertex[2].x =  0.1;
     side_1_vertex[2].y =  0.0;
     side_1_vertex[2].z =  0.1;
     side_1_vertex[3].x =  0.0;
     side_1_vertex[3].y =  0.1;
     side_1_vertex[3].z =  0.1;
     side_1_vertex[4].x = -0.1;
     side_1_vertex[4].y =  0.1;
     side_1_vertex[4].z =  0.1;

    /* Initialize side 2 vertices */
     side_2_vertex[0].x =  0.1;
     side_2_vertex[0].y = -0.1;
     side_2_vertex[0].z =  0.1;
     side_2_vertex[1].x =  0.1;
     side_2_vertex[1].y = -0.1;
     side_2_vertex[1].z = -0.1;
     side_2_vertex[2].x =  0.1;
     side_2_vertex[2].y =  0.0;
     side_2_vertex[2].z = -0.1;
     side_2_vertex[3].x =  0.1;
     side_2_vertex[3].y =  0.0;
     side_2_vertex[3].z =  0.1;
```

```
/* Initialize side 3 vertices */
 side_3_vertex[0].x = -0.1;
 side_3_vertex[0].y = -0.1;
 side_3_vertex[0].z = -0.1;
 side_3_vertex[1].x =  0.1;
 side_3_vertex[1].y = -0.1;
 side_3_vertex[1].z = -0.1;
 side_3_vertex[2].x =  0.1;
 side_3_vertex[2].y =  0.0;
 side_3_vertex[2].z = -0.1;
 side_3_vertex[3].x =  0.0;
 side_3_vertex[3].y =  0.1;
 side_3_vertex[3].z = -0.1;
 side_3_vertex[4].x = -0.1;
 side_3_vertex[4].y =  0.1;
 side_3_vertex[4].z = -0.1;

/* Initialize side 4 vertices */
 side_4_vertex[0].x = -0.1;
 side_4_vertex[0].y = -0.1;
 side_4_vertex[0].z = -0.1;
 side_4_vertex[1].x = -0.1;
 side_4_vertex[1].y = -0.1;
 side_4_vertex[1].z =  0.1;
 side_4_vertex[2].x = -0.1;
 side_4_vertex[2].y =  0.1;
 side_4_vertex[2].z =  0.1;
 side_4_vertex[3].x = -0.1;
 side_4_vertex[3].y =  0.1;
 side_4_vertex[3].z = -0.1;

/* Initialize side 5 vertices */
 side_5_vertex[0].x = -0.1;
 side_5_vertex[0].y =  0.1;
 side_5_vertex[0].z =  0.1;
 side_5_vertex[1].x =  0.0;
 side_5_vertex[1].y =  0.1;
 side_5_vertex[1].z =  0.1;
 side_5_vertex[2].x =  0.0;
 side_5_vertex[2].y =  0.1;
 side_5_vertex[2].z = -0.1;
 side_5_vertex[3].x = -0.1;
 side_5_vertex[3].y =  0.1;
 side_5_vertex[3].z = -0.1;
```

```
/* Initialize side 6 vertices */
 side_6_vertex[0].x = -0.1;
 side_6_vertex[0].y = -0.1;
 side_6_vertex[0].z =  0.1;
 side_6_vertex[1].x =  0.1;
 side_6_vertex[1].y = -0.1;
 side_6_vertex[1].z =  0.1;
 side_6_vertex[2].x =  0.1;
 side_6_vertex[2].y = -0.1;
 side_6_vertex[2].z = -0.1;
 side_6_vertex[3].x = -0.1;
 side_6_vertex[3].y = -0.1;
 side_6_vertex[3].z = -0.1;

/* Initialize side 7 vertices */
 side_7_vertex[0].x =  0.0;
 side_7_vertex[0].y =  0.1;
 side_7_vertex[0].z =  0.1;
 side_7_vertex[1].x =  0.1;
 side_7_vertex[1].y =  0.0;
 side_7_vertex[1].z =  0.1;
 side_7_vertex[2].x =  0.1;
 side_7_vertex[2].y =  0.0;
 side_7_vertex[2].z = -0.1;
 side_7_vertex[3].x =  0.0;
 side_7_vertex[3].y =  0.1;
 side_7_vertex[3].z = -0.1;

/* Set the interior style to solid */
 psetintstyle (PSOLID);

/* Set the color and create a fillarea primitive
  * structure element for each side */
 colour.colour_model = 1;
 colour.colour.x = 1.0;
 colour.colour.y = 0.0;
 colour.colour.z = 0.0;
 psetintcolour (colour);
 pfillarea3 (5, side_1_vertex);

 colour.colour_model = 1;
 colour.colour.x = 0.0;
 colour.colour.y = 1.0;
 colour.colour.z = 0.0;
```

```
psetintcolour (colour);
pfillarea3 (4, side_2_vertex);

colour.colour_model = 1;
colour.colour.x = 0.0;
colour.colour.y = 0.0;
colour.colour.z = 1.0;
psetintcolour (colour);
pfillarea3 (5, side_3_vertex);

colour.colour_model = 1;
colour.colour.x = 1.0;
colour.colour.y = 1.0;
colour.colour.z = 0.0;
psetintcolour (colour);
pfillarea3 (4, side_4_vertex);

colour.colour_model = 1;
colour.colour.x = 1.0;
colour.colour.y = 0.0;
colour.colour.z = 1.0;
psetintcolour (colour);
pfillarea3 (4, side_5_vertex);

colour.colour_model = 1;
colour.colour.x = 0.0;
colour.colour.y = 1.0;
colour.colour.z = 1.0;
psetintcolour (colour);
pfillarea3 (4, side_6_vertex);

colour.colour_model = 1;
colour.colour.x = 0.8;
colour.colour.y = 0.5;
colour.colour.z = 0.2;
psetintcolour (colour);
pfillarea3 (4, side_7_vertex);
}
```

4.4 Color Models

The PHIGS standard provides three other color models as part of the standard in addition to the RGB color model that is used throughout this chapter. The color models that are provided by the PHIGS standard are: Commision Internationale de l'Eclairage (CIE); hue, saturation, value (HSV); red, green, blue (RGB); and hue, lightness, saturation (HLS). While the RGB color model may be the simplest to use, these other models may, for some applications, be more convenient. In this section we shall briefly discuss the RGB and HLS color models. The PHIGS standard documents each of the color models and is a good source of information for study of the other color models.

In Programming Example 4.3, we specified the color model when we defined the direct color attribute. We could have set the color model to any of the PHIGS supported color models by changing the first parameter to the PHIGS function psetpolylinecolour. When using indexed color, we set the color model with the set color model function. This function sets the color model for the entire workstation. Color coordinates specified in the color table are used as coordinates to the specified color model. The default color model may vary, so again, check your individual implementation for the default color model.

Red, Green, Blue

The RGB color model can be described with a simple 3-D coordinate space. Just as we have the X, Y, and Z axes in a standard Cartesian coordinate system, we have the R, G, and B axes in the RGB coordinate system. As you may have guessed, the R axis is red, the G axis is green and the B axes is blue. Each of the axes in the RGB coordinate system, however, extend from 0.0 to 1.0.

Movement along any of the axes produces varying shades of the color of the axes. For example, movement along the Red axis, the X axis, produces varying shades of red. Likewise movement along the Blue or Green axis will produce varying shades of blue or green. A coordinate that is off the axes will produce some combination of colors. For example, the point (0.5, 1.0, 0.0) will produce a color with no blue in it and twice as much green as red. We could plot these coordinates to create the cube that is presented in Figure 4.3. Here we can see the relationships between the different colors we can specify.

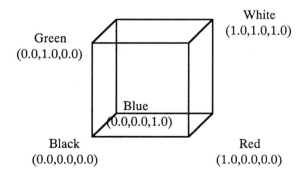

Figure 4.3. RGB color cube.

Just as a painter mixes different ratios of color on his palette to paint on his canvas, we mix different ratios of red, blue and green with which to paint on the display surface. By specifying a point within the color cube, we can mix any ratio of red, green and blue. The point (1.0, 0.0, 1.0) combines a bright red with bright blue to create magenta. We can see that the origin of the RGB coordinate system is black, there is no red, blue or green component to the color. The other end of this spectrum would be point (1.0, 1.0, 1.0), or white, which is the upper-right back corner of the color cube. If we were to move along the line between the black and white coordinate, we would produce varying shades of grey.

Hue, Lightness, Saturation

When specifying a color using the RGB color model, we *mixed* different levels of red, green, and blue to produce on the screen the desired colors. When describing color with the HLS color model, using a value from 0.0 to 1.0 we specify a hue with a saturation and a lightness. The lightness is an intensity or brightness of the color produced.

Just as we had with RGB, we can create a 3-D figure to demonstrate the HLS color model. In Figure 4.4A we have drawn a double-ended color cone. The color coordinates for this model define a point within this cone. The first coordinate, hue, is the angle about the axis of the cone. The second coordinate, light, is the height along the axis which is the intensity of the color. The closer the value of this coordinate is to 1.0, the closer the color is to white. The saturation is the radius from axis. A radius of 1.0 places the coordinate on the outer edge of the cone, while a radius of 0.0 places the point at the center. This is similar to how close on an axes a coordinate was to one in the RGB color model.

When using the RGB color model we specified the color green with the coordinate (0.0, 0.0, 1.0). This coordinate is the lower left back corner of the color cube. To specify that same color green using the HLS color model, we specify a Hue of 125°, a Lightness of 0.5 and a saturation of 1.0. This is shown in Figure 4.4B. We first determine the hue with a radius of 125°. We must now specify the brightness of the color green by specifying the light. A light value of 0.5 gives us a color green that is at the center of the cone. The radius that is the saturation, determines how green the color is. A saturation of 0.1 would give us a very pale green. In the example, we have specified a saturation of 1.0, which gives a fully saturated green color.

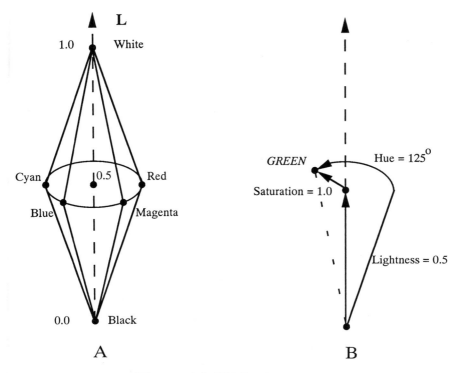

Figure 4.4. HLS color model.

5
Shading and Lighting

Introduction

This chapter introduces the basic concepts necessary for the creation of graphical objects with surface attributes and light sources that affect the appearance of the object's surface. Upon completion of this chapter, the reader will be able to create 3-D graphic objects that appear smooth-shaded. The surface color of a smooth-shaded object is interpolated across the surface. In addition to creating a smooth-shaded object the reader will be able to specify various light sources to produce visual effects which can be used to simulate the real world.

In the examples presented in the previous chapters, we created wireframe and fill area (flat-shaded, nonlighted) objects. While in many applications a wireframe or flat-shaded object may be desired, they are not useful for simulating realistic scenes. We make flat-shaded objects into smooth-shaded objects by providing them with additional surface attributes and polygon vertex information. The addition of a surface, however, introduces a new set of variables with which our application must be concerned. These variables include surface and lighting characteristics.

In Section 5.1 we demonstrate how shading is performed without lighting. To do this, we define, for each vertex of the polygon, a color coordinate. This color coordinate is referred to as the *per-vertex color*. The color of the points on the surface of the object described by these vertices are interpolated across the surface of the polygon from the per-vertex color. For more information on this interpolation process refer to the PHIGS+ Functional Description. In Sections 5.2 and 5.3, we describe shading with light. Shading an object in this manner requires that we specify vertex normals. We will see more of this later in the chapter.

An object's surface can vary from a highly polished bright surface, such as a billiard ball, to an object with a dull matte surface, such as a tennis ball. The difference between these two surfaces is determined by the structure's surface attributes. Section 5.2 discusses these surface attributes and demonstrates how the PHIGS program uses them to create certain effects.

The final step in the display of a solid object is the description of the light in which the object is viewed. The characteristics of the light influence the appearance of the surface of that object. A highly polished white billiard ball viewed in normal room light will appear quite different than that same billiard ball shown under an intense blue spot light. Section 2 of this chapter demonstrates how light sources are created as well as how to set their characteristics to produce a realistic scene.

Light sources and surface properties of an object are input into the *rendering pipeline*. The rendering pipeline is an ordered sequence of calculations whose output is the color value to be drawn on the display surface of the workstation. The input to this pipeline includes the characteristics of the output primitive's surface and the color selected for the output primitive. The rendering pipeline has four stages; lighting, shading, depth cueing, and color approximation.

The lighting and shading stages calculate the surface color of the output primitive based on the light source type and the properties of the output primitive's surface. The interior shading method effects how the calculations for this stage are performed. There are four interior shading methods described in the PHIGS standard; none, color, dot product, and normal. We will describe the effects of these methods in more detail when we discuss Programming Example 5.1.

The depth cueing stage modifies the color of lit and shaded primitives according to the NPC Z coordinate (Chapter 2) of the output primitive. The lit and shaded color rendered by the first two stages of the pipeline is combined with the depth cueing color according to the NPC Z coordinate of output primitive. This produces the effect of the output primitive changing color as it moves away from the viewpoint.

The color approximation stage approximates the color produced by the first three stages of the rendering pipeline. The colors produced by this stage are those that can be displayed on the output device. This stage produces either direct color values or indices into the workstation's color table.

5.1 Shading

In the previous chapter, we defined polygons with a constant color by defining a fill area color. In this chapter, we introduce the concept of shading. The simplest method of smooth shading involves assigning color coordinates to each polygon vertex. The resultant display shows the object with the surface color values interpolated across the surface of the polygon from vertex to vertex. If, for example, we were to draw an equilateral triangle with one vertex blue, one red and one green, the colors on the surface of the triangle would be interpolated among the three such that the center of the triangle would be white. This is known as Gouraud shading.

Shading using vertex colors is useful for defining a shaded object without light sources. It is also useful for the display of physical parameters arranged in an X-Y grid. When working with cartographic data, for example, if the elevation is known for each coordinate, a surface may be defined where the color is a function of the elevation. Lower elevations may be displayed in green, while higher elevations may be displayed in red. The color of the intermediate points will be calculated to be between green and red. The resultant display will resemble a shaded topographic map.

Another example of the use of vertex colors is in the display of certain physical properties such as temperature, pressure, or stress. In computational fluid dynamics (CFD) the pressure measured at various points may be defined as vertex colors to visually display flow fields.

Programming Example 5.1

Programming Example 5.1 is, for the most part, a duplication of Programming Example 4.1. Just as in Programming Example 4.1, we open PHIGS and a workstation. When we open the workstation, we specify that it is to be an output true-color workstation by setting the type to PWST_OUTPUT_TRUE. As you will recall from Chapter 1, this opens an output device with true-color capability. After the workstation is opened, a structure is opened. The subroutine create_shaded_object is called. This subroutine creates a smooth-shaded object without using any light sources. The subroutine then sets the interior shading method to PSH_COLOUR, which tells PHIGS that we are using either normals or per-vertex colors to shade the surface of the object.

The create_shaded_object subroutine then defines the object as a solid object that is to have hidden lines and surfaces removed (Chapter 4). We then create a structure element that contains the per-vertex colors. This tells PHIGS that we are using the per-vertex color method of shading as opposed to the vertex normal method of shading, which is described in the next section.

In the previous chapter, we created a solid object by using the pfillarea3 function call. In this example, we will use the pfillarea3data function call. The difference between the two functions is that pfillarea3data assigns data to each vertex in addition to the vertex coordinates. The limitation of the pfillarea3 function is that the shading across the surface of the polygon is constant (flat shaded), and there is not enough information to smooth shade the object. The pfillarea3data function provides the ability to associate data with the vertices to smooth shade and light the object.

The remainder of the example program uses functions and subroutines to rotate and view the object. The functions and subroutines have been discussed previously in the text. Refer to Chapter 4 for information on these calls.

Set Interior Lighting Method

The interior lighting method determines the types of light that are considered as part of the lighting calculations. The following PHIGS function call creates a

Table 5.1. Interior lighting methods.

Type	Description
≤ 0	Implementation dependent
1	No lighting calculations performed
2	Ambient light
3	Ambient and diffuse light
4	Ambient, diffuse, and specular light
≥ 5	Reserved

structure element that sets the lighting method used for the subsequent output primitives:

```
psetintlightmethod (1);      /*(PHOP,*,STOP,*)*/
```

The function receives as input an integer value describing the types of light that are to be considered as part of the lighting equation. In this example, we have not used any lighting in order to demonstrate smooth-shading using per-vertex color. In the next section, we will discuss the use of the other lighting methods. The acceptable values according to the PHIGS standard for this parameter are described in Table 5.1.

Set Interior Shade Method

The interior shading method affects how the calculations for the lighting and shading stages of the rendering pipeline are performed. There are four interior shading methods described in the PHIGS standard: none, color, dot product, and normal. The following PHIGS function call creates a structure element that sets the interior shading method:

```
psetintshademethod (PSH_COLOUR);
                        /*(PHOP,*,STOP,*)*/
```

The function receives as input an integer value describing the interior shading method. The acceptable values according to the PHIGS standard for this parameter are described in Table 5.2.

Table 5.2. Interior shading method.

Type	Description
≤ 0	Implementation-dependent
1	None
2	Color
3	Dot product
4	Normal
≥ 5	Reserved

When using no interior shading method, none, the interior of the polygon is filled with a single color determined by the current interior attributes. In the example, using color (PSH_COLOUR) denotes either per-vertex, and/or normal data are supplied with the FILL AREA 3 WITH DATA primitive.

Fill Area 3 with Data

When the interior shading method is set to color, the PHIGS program must supply per-vertex color coordinates and/or vertex normals. In this example we are demonstrating the use of per-vertex colors. Programming Example 5.2 will demonstrate the use of vertex normals. The following function call provides PHIGS with the per-vertex color information:

```
pfillarea3data (PFA_NONE, PVERT_COLOUR,
         PCM_RGB, &fadata, 5, &vdata);
                /*(PHOP,*,STOP,*)*/
```

The function receives as input the fill area flag which is an integer indicating whether or not a single normal (geometric normal) will be used to define the entire area. In this example, we wish to use vertex information, PFA_NONE. This indicates that we do not regard the polygon as having a flat-shaded color or geometric normal. A geometric normal implies a flat surface; refer to the PHIGS standard for further information concerning a geometric normal and its relationship to a surface.

The second parameter to the function, the vertex flag, indicates what information is specified for each vertex in the vdata data structure. *STOP AND THINK ABOUT THIS.* A value of PVERT_COLOUR indicates color coordinates and vertex coordinates. As this value changes, so do the data associated with each vertex. The third parameter specifies the color mode. In the example we have used the RGB color model.

The fourth parameter is the fill area data. In the example this data structure is ignored because the fill area flag has been set to none. If the fill area flag had been set to specify a geometric normal, the fadata structure would define a geometric normal for the entire polygon.

The fifth parameter to the function call is the number of vertices describing the polygon. In the example, the polygons are defined as having either four or five vertices.

The final parameter to the function call is a structure containing the information for each vertex. The actual structure of this parameter is dependent on the data type indicated by the vertex flag. Refer to the above description of the vertex flag. In the example, we have specified the vertex flag as coordinate and color values. The structure of vdata, therefore, contains vertex coordinates and color coordinates. Check the documentation of your implementation to determine the possible vdata structures.

```
/*
 *                              Example 5.1
 */
#include <phigs.h>

#define WS_ID              1
#define STRUCT_ID          1
#define VIEW_ID            1
#define CHILD_ID           2
#define LABEL              1


main()
{
    Pint        i;
    Ppoint3     pt;
    Pvector3    shift;
    Pvector3    scale;
    Pfloat      angle;
    Pmatrix3    matrix;
    Pint        error;

    /* initialize rotation setting */
    angle = 0.0;

    /* initialize center of object, shift
                                vector and scale */
    pt.x    = 0.0;
    pt.y    = 0.0;
    pt.z    = 0.0;
    shift.x = 0.0;
    shift.y = 0.0;
    shift.z = 0.0;
    scale.x = 1.0;
    scale.y = 1.0;
    scale.z = 1.0;

    /* Open PHIGS */
    popenphigs ("/dev/tty", 0);

    /* Open a true-color workstation */
    popenws (WS_ID, 0, PWST_OUTPUT_TRUE);

    /* Define a view for the workstation */
    define_angle_view (WS_ID, VIEW_ID);
```

```
/* Set HLHSR mode This turns on z-buffering for
 * the workstation */
psethlhsrmode (WS_ID, 1);

/* Open a parent structure */
popenstruct (STRUCT_ID);

/* Set HLHSR ID This turns on Z-buffering for
 * this structure */
psethlhsrid (1);

/* Set the view index */
psetviewind (VIEW_ID);

/* Create an axis */
create_axis ();

/* Set a label
 * This serves as a pointer to the following
 * structure element */
plabel (LABEL);

/* Initialize matrix to identity (normal) - No
 * structure element is created, just a matrix
 * in main memory */
identity3 (matrix);

/* Set the identity matrix as the local
 * transformation matrix. A structure element is
 * created.  The label is therefore just before
 * this structure element.  Later we will come
 * back to edit this structure element
 * containing the set local transform element */
psetlocaltran3 (matrix, PREPLACE);

/* Execute the child structure  The child
 * structure will be created later. Nothing will
 * be executed until the structure network is
 * traversed (using predrawallstruct or
 * pupdatews).  We cannot create child structure
 * now because we already have a structure open.
 * When executed, the child structure will
 * inherit the above transformation and view
 * from the parent. */
pexecutestruct (CHILD_ID);
```

```
/* Close the structure */
pclosestruct ();

/* Open the child structure */
popenstruct (STRUCT_ID);

/* Draw the object */
create_shaded_object ();

/* Close the child structure */
pclosestruct ();

/* Post the parent structure to the workstation
 * Note: only the parent structure is posted.
 * The child structure will be executed by the
 * parent. */
ppoststruct (WS_ID, STRUCT_ID, 0.0);

/*Redraw all structures posted to
 *                the workstation */
predrawallstruct (WS_ID, PALWAYS);

/* Set edit mode to replace This will put all
 * succeding calls into the same place  in DLM
 * so that just the one set local transformation
 * instruction will be changed (Note: a common
 * mistake is  to forget to reset edit mode to
 * INSERT before defining a new structure,
 * resulting in a structure which contains
 * nothing) */
pseteditmode (PEDIT_REPLACE);

/* Open parent structure so it can be edited */
popenstruct (STRUCT_ID);

/* Set the element pointer to the beginning of
 * the parent structure - the pointer will be at
 * the end of the structure if you don't reset
 * it to the beginning */
psetelemptr (0);

/* Set the element pointer to the label - This
 * points to the label, to replace the local
 * matrix the pointer will have to be offset to
```

```
 * the next element in the structure */
psetelemptrlabel (LABEL);

/* Offset the element pointer to point to the
 * local transformation */
poffsetelemptr (1);

/* Now we are pointing to the set local
 * transform structure element in the structure
 * network.  We'll loop, changing  the
 * translation vector each loop to move the
 * object around  the origin in a circular
 * fashion. A translation matrix is created that
 * replaces the previous local matrix in the
 * structure network.  The structure network is
 * retraversed to show the object in its new
 * position */

/* Do for awhile */
for (i=0; i<100; i++)
    {
    /* Increment rotation values */
    angle = angle + 0.1;

    /* Build transformation matrix */
    pbuildtran3 (&pt, &shift, angle, angle,
            angle, &scale, &error, matrix);

    /* Set the local transformation matrix -
     * This is the structure element to be
     * replaced */
    psetlocaltran3 (matrix, PPRECONCATENATE);

    /* Redraw all structures - This will redraw
     * all structures posted to the
     * workstation*/
    predrawallstruct (WS_ID, PALWAYS);

    /* Sleep */
    sleep (1);
    }
/* End do */

/* Close the structure that was open for editing
 * This is often  forgotten, creating a state
```

```
     * error when trying to open another
     * structure */
    pclosestruct ();

    /* Set edit mode to INSERT - Although this it
     * not necessary in this example (as no more
     * structure creation will take place), it is a
     * good idea to get into the habit of always re-
     * setting the edit mode to INSERT (the
     * default).  Forgetting to do so will cause
     * problems later in more complex programs.  You
     * will be in a situation where every structure
     * element is overwritten, creating structures
     * containing nothing */
    pseteditmode (PEDIT_INSERT);

    /* Close the workstation */
    pclosews (WS_ID);

    /* Close PHIGS */
    pclosephigs ();
}


create_shaded_object ()
{
#include <phigs.h>

    Pptco3        vertex_data[5];
    Pfasdata3     fadata;
    Pfasvdata3    vdata;

    /* Apply no lighting */
    psetintlightmethod (1);

    /* Use color information for shading */
    psetintshademethod (PSH_COLOUR);

    /* Make the surface solid */
    psetintstyle (PSOLID);

    /* Apply hidden-line/hidden-surface removal */
    psethlhsrid (1);

    /* Initialize vertex colors. We'll put a
     * different color in each vertex on each side.
```

```
     * We'll use the same colors  for each side. */
    vertex_data[0].colour.x =  1.0;
    vertex_data[0].colour.y =  0.0;
    vertex_data[0].colour.z =  0.0;
    vertex_data[1].colour.x =  0.0;
    vertex_data[1].colour.y =  1.0;
    vertex_data[1].colour.z =  0.0;
    vertex_data[2].colour.x =  0.0;
    vertex_data[2].colour.y =  0.0;
    vertex_data[2].colour.z =  1.0;
    vertex_data[3].colour.x =  1.0;
    vertex_data[3].colour.y =  1.0;
    vertex_data[3].colour.z =  0.0;
    vertex_data[4].colour.x =  1.0;
    vertex_data[4].colour.y =  0.0;
    vertex_data[4].colour.z =  1.0;

  /* Initialize side 1 vertices */
   vertex_data[0].point.x = -0.1;
   vertex_data[0].point.y = -0.1;
   vertex_data[0].point.z =  0.1;
   vertex_data[1].point.x =  0.1;
   vertex_data[1].point.y = -0.1;
   vertex_data[1].point.z =  0.1;
   vertex_data[2].point.x =  0.1;
   vertex_data[2].point.y =  0.0;
   vertex_data[2].point.z =  0.1;
   vertex_data[3].point.x =  0.0;
   vertex_data[3].point.y =  0.1;
   vertex_data[3].point.z =  0.1;
   vertex_data[4].point.x = -0.1;
   vertex_data[4].point.y =  0.1;
   vertex_data[4].point.z =  0.1;

   /* Put the coordinate and color values into a
    * data structure */
   vdata.ptco = vertex_data;

   /* Output side 1 */
   pfillarea3data (PFA_NONE, PVERT_COLOUR,
       PCM_RGB, &fadata, 5, &vdata);

  /* Initialize side 2 vertices */
   vertex_data[0].point.x =  0.1;
   vertex_data[0].point.y = -0.1;
```

```
vertex_data[0].point.z =   0.1;
vertex_data[1].point.x =   0.1;
vertex_data[1].point.y =  -0.1;
vertex_data[1].point.z =  -0.1;
vertex_data[2].point.x =   0.1;
vertex_data[2].point.y =   0.0;
vertex_data[2].point.z =  -0.1;
vertex_data[3].point.x =   0.1;
vertex_data[3].point.y =   0.0;
vertex_data[3].point.z =   0.1;

/* Put the coordinate and color values into a
 * data structure */
vdata.ptco = vertex_data;

/* Output side 2 */
pfillarea3data (PFA_NONE, PVERT_COLOUR,
    PCM_RGB, &fadata, 4, &vdata);

/* Initialize side 3 vertices */
vertex_data[0].point.x =  -0.1;
vertex_data[0].point.y =  -0.1;
vertex_data[0].point.z =  -0.1;
vertex_data[1].point.x =   0.1;
vertex_data[1].point.y =  -0.1;
vertex_data[1].point.z =  -0.1;
vertex_data[2].point.x =   0.1;
vertex_data[2].point.y =   0.0;
vertex_data[2].point.z =  -0.1;
vertex_data[3].point.x =   0.0;
vertex_data[3].point.y =   0.1;
vertex_data[3].point.z =  -0.1;
vertex_data[4].point.x =  -0.1;
vertex_data[4].point.y =   0.1;
vertex_data[4].point.z =  -0.1;

/* Put the coordinate and color values into a
 * data structure */
vdata.ptco = vertex_data;

/* Output side 3 */
pfillarea3data (PFA_NONE, PVERT_COLOUR,
    PCM_RGB, &fadata, 5, &vdata);
```

```
/* Initialize side 4 vertices */
vertex_data[0].point.x = -0.1;
vertex_data[0].point.y = -0.1;
vertex_data[0].point.z = -0.1;
vertex_data[1].point.x = -0.1;
vertex_data[1].point.y = -0.1;
vertex_data[1].point.z =  0.1;
vertex_data[2].point.x = -0.1;
vertex_data[2].point.y =  0.1;
vertex_data[2].point.z =  0.1;
vertex_data[3].point.x = -0.1;
vertex_data[3].point.y =  0.1;
vertex_data[3].point.z = -0.1;

/* Put the coordinate and color values into a
 * data structure */
vdata.ptco = vertex_data;

/* Output side 4 */
pfillarea3data (PFA_NONE, PVERT_COLOUR,
    PCM_RGB, &fadata, 4, &vdata);

/* Initialize side 5 vertices */
vertex_data[0].point.x = -0.1;
vertex_data[0].point.y =  0.1;
vertex_data[0].point.z =  0.1;
vertex_data[1].point.x =  0.0;
vertex_data[1].point.y =  0.1;
vertex_data[1].point.z =  0.1;
vertex_data[2].point.x =  0.0;
vertex_data[2].point.y =  0.1;
vertex_data[2].point.z = -0.1;
vertex_data[3].point.x = -0.1;
vertex_data[3].point.y =  0.1;
vertex_data[3].point.z = -0.1;

/* Put the coordinate and color values into a
 * data structure */
vdata.ptco = vertex_data;

/* Output side 5 */
pfillarea3data (PFA_NONE, PVERT_COLOUR,
    PCM_RGB, &fadata, 4, &vdata);
```

```
/* Initialize side 6 vertices */
vertex_data[0].point.x = -0.1;
vertex_data[0].point.y = -0.1;
vertex_data[0].point.z =  0.1;
vertex_data[1].point.x =  0.1;
vertex_data[1].point.y = -0.1;
vertex_data[1].point.z =  0.1;
vertex_data[2].point.x =  0.1;
vertex_data[2].point.y = -0.1;
vertex_data[2].point.z = -0.1;
vertex_data[3].point.x = -0.1;
vertex_data[3].point.y = -0.1;
vertex_data[3].point.z = -0.1;

/* Put the coordinate and color values into a
 * data structure */
vdata.ptco = vertex_data;

/* Output side 6 */
pfillarea3data (PFA_NONE, PVERT_COLOUR,
    PCM_RGB, &fadata, 4, &vdata);

/* Initialize side 7 vertices */
vertex_data[0].point.x =  0.0;
vertex_data[0].point.y =  0.1;
vertex_data[0].point.z =  0.1;
vertex_data[1].point.x =  0.1;
vertex_data[1].point.y =  0.0;
vertex_data[1].point.z =  0.1;
vertex_data[2].point.x =  0.1;
vertex_data[2].point.y =  0.0;
vertex_data[2].point.z = -0.1;
vertex_data[3].point.x =  0.0;
vertex_data[3].point.y =  0.1;
vertex_data[3].point.z = -0.1;

/* Put the coordinate and color values into a
 * data structure */
vdata.ptco = vertex_data;

/* Output side 7 */
pfillarea3data (PFA_NONE, PVERT_COLOUR,
    PCM_RGB, &fadata, 4, &vdata);
}
```

5.2 Surface Features and Shading

Surface characteristics determine how light is reflected by an object. In addition to reflected light, surface attributes determine the amount of light that passes through the object, that is the transparency of the object. The program tells PHIGS the characteristics of an object by specifying the surface attributes. In this section, we shall discuss these attributes and demonstrate how they are used by a PHIGS program.

There are three different types of light reflected by a surface: ambient, specular, and diffuse. To create surfaces that reflect light differently in PHIGS, we vary the ratios of these light types reflected by the surface. *Ambient light* is light that comes from all directions. Ambient light provides a constant illumination on all surfaces of an object regardless of their orientation or position.

Specular light and *diffuse light* are opposite ends of the same range. A surface that is highly specular reflects light in one direction. This is shown in Figure 5.1. An example of a surface that is completely specular is a ball with a mirror surface. If a spot light strikes the ball, all the light is reflected at the same angle. In contrast, a diffuse surface will scatter the reflected light at different angles. An example of a more diffuse surface would be an apple. The reflected light is spread over a larger surface of the sphere. A more diffuse sphere would be a tennis ball; the reflected light is evenly distributed across the entire surface of the sphere.

When describing the actual surface of an object, we shall specify how much of each of these types of light the object will reflect. In the following programming example, we will demonstrate how to create a surface with these reflective characteristics. This example is presented as a subroutine so that it may be used as part of a library of user written subroutines for actual applications.

The characteristics of the light with which we view an object influence the appearance of the surface of that object. A highly polished billiard ball viewed in normal room light will appear quite different than that same billiard ball shown under an intense blue spotlight. In this section we shall also discuss how to define light sources in which the object is viewed.

The light reflected by the surface of an object emanates from a light source. Just as in the real world, an object may reflect the light from many light sources at one time. These light sources are defined for a workstation in a workstation light table in the workstation state list. When a structure is posted to a workstation it activates the light sources from this table that are to affect the object displayed on the workstation. The maximum size of the workstation light table may vary between implementations.

There are four types of light sources that may be defined in the workstations light table: ambient, infinite, point, and spot. Ambient light is the least compute intensive form of light allowed by PHIGS, since all points on the surface of the object are illuminated by the light source in the same way. Ambient light is

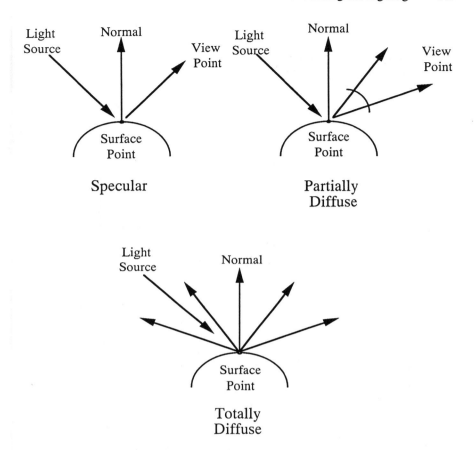

Figure 5.1. Specular-diffuse light types.

independent of the surface being lit or the location of the eye. This is the same type of ambient light that was described above. It is the light that is present without emanating from a particular light source. When working with ambient light, we need only define the color of the light.

An *infinite light* source requires slightly more computation than ambient light. The light rays emanating from an infinite light source are parallel. As we know all parallel lines meet at infinity, the position of an infinite light source, therefore, is at infinity. Since the rays of light are parallel, they strike each point of the surface at the same angle. This greatly simplifies the calculations. Although there are no examples of a literally infinite light source in the real world, the sun is virtually an infinite light source. The distance of the sun makes the angle between the light rays very small. When working with an infinite light source, we need only define the color of the light and the direction of light rays.

A *point light* source is the next most compute intensive because the rays of light emanating from the source strike the points on the surface of the object at different angles. This requires color computations to be performed for every point on the surface. If we were to look at a white billiard ball under a red light, the color of the ball would be affected by the ball's distance from the red light. The closer the ball is to the point light, the greater the influence of the color of that light on the surface of an object. The strength of this influence is specified by the *attenuation coefficient*. The attenuation coefficient controls how much the light source weakens in relation to the distance of the object from the source of light. When working with a point light source, we must specify the color of the light source, the position of the light source, and the attenuation coefficient.

A *spotlight* source is the most computationally intense form of light. A spotlight source has a color, position, direction, *concentration exponent*, attenuation coefficient, and a *spread angle*. The color of a surface point is scaled by the cosine of the angle between the light source direction and the line from the point of the light source and the point on the surface. This color is raised to the concentration exponent power. The concentration exponent controls the change in the strength of the light from the center of the cone to the edge. The spread angle determines the diameter of the cone. The closer we are to the center of the cone the stronger the influence of the light is on the color of the surface point. If a surface point is outside the cone of influence, it is not affected by the lighting calculation for the light source.

We see an example of a spotlight source in Figure 5.2. Here we have created a light with a cone of influence, spread angle, of 25°. Within that cone, there is point A, which is at a 30° angle to the direction of the light. The color of point A is scaled by the cosine of 30°. The color is then raised to the concentration exponent, which provides a variance of color between the point and the center of the cone of influence. We see that point B is not affected by the spotlight because it is outside the cone of influence. We can see that a spotlight affects the color of a point in two dimensions, first the attenuation, the distance from the light, affects the color of the point. Second, the color of the point is affected by the distance of the point from the center of the cone of influence. It is important to experiment with the different parameters of this light source to observe the visual differences.

Programming Example 5.2

Programming Example 5.2 demonstrates how to specify the surface properties of an object and light sources by which the object is lit. This program is similar to Programming Example 5.1. In Example 5.2, however, the program calls the user subroutines define_surface and define_lighting. The define_surface subroutine performs the same surface functions as demonstrated in Example 5.1. In addition the subroutine sets the surface properties and interior color index. The define_lighting subroutine defines ambient, infinite, point, and spotlight sources.

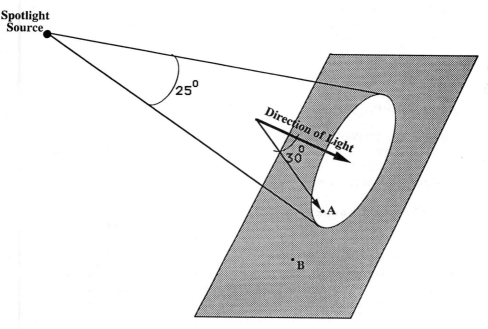

Figure 5.2. Spotlight source.

The light sources with position and/or direction are defined to be directly above the object being lit.

The program then calls the user subroutine create_lighted_object. This subroutine is similar to the user subroutine create_shaded_object, except that vertex normals are defined in addition to per-vertex colors. You will notice that create_lighted_object supplies per vertex colors and geometric normals. They will not be used by the example, however, due to the setting of PSH_COLOUR in psetintshademethod, which is called by define_source. The rest of the program performs the same animation as used throughout Chapters 4 and 5.

Set Interior Lighting Method

The interior lighting method determines the types of light that are considered as part of the lighting calculations. The following PHIGS function call creates a structure element that sets the lighting method used for the subsequent output primitives:

```
psetintlightmethod (light_method);
                           /*(PHOP,*,STOP,*)*/
```

The function receives as input an integer value describing the types of light that are to be considered as part of the lighting equation. In the previous section we specified that no light sources were to be used. In this example we have specified that the ambient, diffuse, and specular light sources are to be used in the shading calculations.

Set Surface Properties

The reflective properties of the surface itself determine how the object appears on the display in relation to the light in which the object is viewed. The following PHIGS function call sets the surface properties of the structure's subsequent output primitives:

psetsurfprop (&surf_prop);

/*(PHOP,*,STOP,*)*/

The function receives as input values for the ambient light coefficient, diffuse light coefficient, specular light coefficient, the specular color, specular exponent, and transparency of the surface. The implementation presented in the examples groups these input parameters together into a single record of type Psurfprop. The standard specifies only that these input parameters be floating point values and not necessarily a record. Check your individual implementation for the correct order and type of parameters to pass to this function call.

The ambient, diffuse, and specular light coefficients have a range of 0.0 to 1.0. They control the brightness of the surface reflection of each of the respective light types. A surface with a 1.0 for diffuse light would have a very dull matte surface, while a surface with a 1.0 for specular light would have a bright highlight on the surface. Each of these values can be independently manipulated, therefore, it is recommended that the reader experiment with different combinations of these values to see firsthand what effect they have on the surface of the object.

Specular color is a color coordinate that specifies the color of the specular light. The color of the specular light need not be the same color as the surface of the object. For example, a white light can shine on a red billiard ball producing a white spot on the surface of the ball. The color model of the specular light is set with the PHIGS function call set rendering color model (not shown in this example).

The specular exponent determines the shine of the surface of the object. The higher the specular exponent of the surface of the object, the shinier the surface of the object. The specular exponent is a floating point value that is greater than 0.0.

Transparency is a real value in the range of 0.0 to 1.0. The transparency coefficient controls the amount of light that passes through the object. A high transparency coefficient creates a transparent object. The closer the transparency coefficient is to 0.0, the more opaque is the object.

Creating a Lighted Object

The subroutine create_lighted_object is similar to the user subroutine create_shaded_object with the addition of vertex normals. We provide this information via the pfillarea3data function call as we did in the previous example. Refer to Section 5.1 for a more detailed description of this function call. We have changed the vertex flag in the function call to PVERT_COLOURNORMAL, which indicates that the vdata structure contains both per-vertex color and *vertex normals*. The vertex normal is perpendicular to the surface at the vertex. The rendering pipeline uses these vertex normals to calculate the angle at which light sources strike the object.

The vertex normals are specified as vectors relative to the vertex coordinates. In Figure 5.3 vertex normal A represents one of the normals for the front facing side. This side of the object is defined to be parallel to the X-Y plane. A perpendicular to this plane is, therefore, parallel to the Z axis and pointing in a positive direction. Since perpendiculars are relative to the vertices and because this is a flat surface, each of the vertex normals for this side will have the same value (0.0, 0.0, 1.0). Vertex normal B represents one of the normals for the right facing side. This side of the object is defined to be parallel to the Y-Z plane. A perpendicular to this plane is, therefore, parallel to the X axis pointing in a positive direction and has a value of (0.0, 1.0, 0.0).

Vertex normal C represents a normal for the diagonal side of the object. This side is at an angle of 135°. The normal for this side is 45° (135-90). The vertex normal may be calculated as follows:

$$\text{Vertex Normal}_x = \text{Cos } 45^{\circ};$$

$$\text{Vertex Normal}_y = \text{Sin } 45^{\circ}.$$

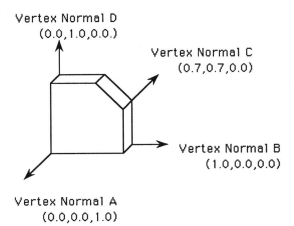

Figure 5.3. Vertex normals.

The Z value is left at zero because the vertex normal is perpendicular to the Z plane.

The perpendicular to this plane then points directly toward the viewer along the positive Z axis. Due to the fact that the surface is parallel to the X-Y plane, the vertex normal does not change.

```
/*
 *                                  Example 5.2
 */
#include <phigs.h>

#define WS_ID           1
#define STRUCT_ID       1
#define VIEW_ID         1
#define CHILD_ID        2
#define LABEL           1

main()
{
    Pint        i;
    Ppoint3     pt;
    Pvector3    shift;
    Pvector3    scale;
    Pfloat      angle;
    Pmatrix3    matrix;
    Pint        error;

    /* Initialize rotation setting */
    angle = 0.0;

    /* Initialize center of object, shift vector
     * and scale */
    pt.x    = 0.0;
    pt.y    = 0.0;
    pt.z    = 0.0;
    shift.x = 0.0;
    shift.y = 0.0;
    shift.z = 0.0;
    scale.x = 1.0;
    scale.y = 1.0;
    scale.z = 1.0;
```

```
/* Open PHIGS */
popenphigs ("/dev/tty", 0);

/* Open a true-color workstation */
popenws (WS_ID, 0, PWST_OUTPUT_TRUE);

/* Define a view for the workstation */
define_angle_view (WS_ID, VIEW_ID);

/* Set HLHSR mode This turns on z-buffering for
 * the workstation */
psethlhsrmode (WS_ID, 1);

/* Open a parent structure */
popenstruct (STRUCT_ID);

/* Set HLHSR ID - This turns on Z-buffering for
 * this structure */
psethlhsrid (1);

/* Set the view index */
psetviewind (VIEW_ID);

/* Create an axis */
create_axis ();

/* Set a label - This serves as a pointer to the
 * following structure element */
plabel (LABEL);

/* Initialize matrix to identity (normal) - No
 * structure element is created, just a matrix
 * in main memory */
identity3 (matrix);

/* Set the identity matrix as the local
 * transformation matrix A structure element is
 * created.  The label is therefore just
 * before this structure element. Later we will
 * come back to edit this structure element
 * containing the set local transform element */
psetlocaltran3 (matrix, PREPLACE);
```

```
/* Execute the child structure -
 * The child structure will be created later.
 * Nothing will be executed until the structure
 * network is traversed (using predrawallstruct
 * or pupdatews).  We cannot create child
 * structure now because we already have a
 * structure Open. When executed, the child
 * structure will inherit the above
 * transformation and view from the parent. */
pexecutestruct (CHILD_ID);

/* Close the structure */
pclosestruct ();

/* Open the child structure */
popenstruct (STRUCT_ID);

/* Define surface characteristics */
define_surface
    (1, 4, PSH_COLOUR, PSOLID);

/* Define light sources */
define_lighting (WS_ID);

/* Draw the object */




create_lighted_object ();

/* Close the child structure */
pclosestruct ();

/* Post the parent structure to the workstation
 * Note: only the parent structure is posted.
 * The child structure will be executed by the
 * parent. */
ppoststruct (WS_ID, STRUCT_ID, 0.0);

/* Redraw all structures posted to the
 * workstation */
predrawallstruct (WS_ID, PALWAYS);
```

```
/* Set edit mode to replace  This will put all
 * succeding calls into the same place in DLM so
 * that just the one Set local transformation
 * instruction will be changed (Note: a common
 * mistake is to forget to reset edit mode to
 * INSERT before defining a new structure,
 * resulting in a structure which contains
 * nothing) */
pseteditmode (PEDIT_REPLACE);

/* Open parent structure so it can be edited */
popenstruct (STRUCT_ID);

/* Set the element pointer to the beginning of
 * the parent structure - the pointer will be at
 * the end of the structure  if you don't reset
 * it to the beginning */
psetelemptr (0);

/* Set the element pointer to the label - This
 * points to the label, to replace the local
 * matrix the pointer will have to be offset to
 * the next element in the structure */
psetelemptrlabel (LABEL);

/* Offset the element pointer to point to the
 * local transformation */
poffsetelemptr (1);

/* Now we are pointing to the Set local
 * transform structure element in the structure
 * network.  We'll loop, changing the
 * translation vector each loop to move the
 * object around the origin in a circular
 * fashion.  A translation matrix is created
 * which replaces the previous local matrix in
 * the structure network.  The structure network
 * is re-traversed to show the object in it's
 * new position */

/* Do for a while */
for (i=0; i<100; i++)
    {
    /* Increment rotation values */
```

```
        angle = angle + 0.1;

        /* Build transformation matrix */
        pbuildtran3 (&pt, &shift, angle, angle,
                      angle, &scale, &error, matrix);

        /* Set the local transformation matrix -
         * This is the structure element to be
         * replaced */
        psetlocaltran3 (matrix, PPRECONCATENATE);

        /* Redraw all structures - This will redraw
         * all structures posted to the
         * workstation*/
        predrawallstruct (WS_ID, PALWAYS);

        /* Sleep */
        sleep (1);
        }
/* End do */

/* Close the structure that was Open for editing
 * This is often forgotten, creating a state
 * error when trying to Open another structure*/
pclosestruct ();

/* Set edit mode to insert - Although this it
 * not necessary in this example (as no more
 * structure creation will take place), it is a
 * good idea to get into the habit of always
 * re-setting the edit mode to insert (the
 * default).  Forgetting to do so will cause
 * problems later in more complex programs.
 * You will be in a situation where every
 * structure element is overwritten, creating
 * structures containing nothing */
pseteditmode (PEDIT_INSERT);

/* Close the workstation */
pclosews (WS_ID);

/* Close PHIGS */
pclosephigs ();
}
```

```
create_lighted_object ()
{
#include <phigs.h>

    Pint         i;
    Ppoint3      vertex[5];
    Pvector3     normal[5],      geonorm;
    Pptconorm3   ptnorm[5];
    Pfasdata3    fadata;
    Pfasvdata3   vdata;
    Pcobundl     vcolour;

    /* Initialize vertex color structure */
    vcolour.x = 1.0;
    vcolour.y = 0.0;
    vcolour.z = 0.0;
    for (i=0; i<5; i++)
      {
      ptnorm[i].colour = vcolour;
      }

    /* Initialize side 1 vertices */
    ptnorm[0].point.x = -0.1;
    ptnorm[0].point.y = -0.1;
    ptnorm[0].point.z =  0.1;
    ptnorm[1].point.x =  0.1;
    ptnorm[1].point.y = -0.1;
    ptnorm[1].point.z =  0.1;
    ptnorm[2].point.x =  0.1;
    ptnorm[2].point.y =  0.0;
    ptnorm[2].point.z =  0.1;
    ptnorm[3].point.x =  0.0;
    ptnorm[3].point.y =  0.1;
    ptnorm[3].point.z =  0.1;
    ptnorm[4].point.x = -0.1;
    ptnorm[4].point.y =  0.1;
    ptnorm[4].point.z =  0.1;
    ptnorm[0].normal.x =  0.0;
    ptnorm[0].normal.y =  0.0;
    ptnorm[0].normal.z =  1.0;
    ptnorm[1].normal.x =  0.0;
    ptnorm[1].normal.y =  0.0;
    ptnorm[1].normal.z =  1.0;
    ptnorm[2].normal.x =  0.0;
    ptnorm[2].normal.y =  0.0;
```

```
ptnorm[2].normal.z =   1.0;
ptnorm[3].normal.x =   0.0;
ptnorm[3].normal.y =   0.0;
ptnorm[3].normal.z =   1.0;
ptnorm[4].normal.x =   0.0;
ptnorm[4].normal.y =   0.0;
ptnorm[4].normal.z =   1.0;

/* Determine and save the fill area normals */
geonorm.x = ptnorm[0].normal.x;
geonorm.y = ptnorm[0].normal.y;
geonorm.z = ptnorm[0].normal.z;
fadata.gnormal = geonorm;

/* Put the coordinate and color values into a
 * data structure */
vdata.ptconorm = ptnorm;

/* Output side 1 */
pfillarea3data (PFA_NORMAL, PVERT_COLOURNORMAL,
    PCM_RGB, &fadata, 5, &vdata);

/* Initialize side 2 vertices */
ptnorm[0].point.x =   0.1;
ptnorm[0].point.y =  -0.1;
ptnorm[0].point.z =   0.1;
ptnorm[1].point.x =   0.1;
ptnorm[1].point.y =  -0.1;
ptnorm[1].point.z =  -0.1;
ptnorm[2].point.x =   0.1;
ptnorm[2].point.y =   0.0;
ptnorm[2].point.z =  -0.1;
ptnorm[3].point.x =   0.1;
ptnorm[3].point.y =   0.0;
ptnorm[3].point.z =   0.1;
ptnorm[0].normal.x =   1.0;
ptnorm[0].normal.y =   0.0;
ptnorm[0].normal.z =   0.0;
ptnorm[1].normal.x =   1.0;
ptnorm[1].normal.y =   0.0;
ptnorm[1].normal.z =   0.0;
ptnorm[2].normal.x =   1.0;
ptnorm[2].normal.y =   0.0;
ptnorm[2].normal.z =   0.0;
ptnorm[3].normal.x =   1.0;
```

```
ptnorm[3].normal.y =   0.0;
ptnorm[3].normal.z =   0.0;

/* Determine and save the fill area normals */
geonorm.x = ptnorm[0].normal.x;
geonorm.y = ptnorm[0].normal.y;
geonorm.z = ptnorm[0].normal.z;
fadata.gnormal = geonorm;

/* Put the coordinate and color values into a
 * data structure */
vdata.ptconorm = ptnorm;

/* Output side 2 */
pfillarea3data (PFA_NORMAL, PVERT_COLOURNORMAL,
    PCM_RGB, &fadata, 4, &vdata);

/* Initialize side 3 vertices */
ptnorm[0].point.x = -0.1;
ptnorm[0].point.y = -0.1;
ptnorm[0].point.z = -0.1;
ptnorm[1].point.x =  0.1;
ptnorm[1].point.y = -0.1;
ptnorm[1].point.z = -0.1;
ptnorm[2].point.x =  0.1;
ptnorm[2].point.y =  0.0;
ptnorm[2].point.z = -0.1;
ptnorm[3].point.x =  0.0;
ptnorm[3].point.y =  0.1;
ptnorm[3].point.z = -0.1;
ptnorm[4].point.x = -0.1;
ptnorm[4].point.y =  0.1;
ptnorm[4].point.z = -0.1;
ptnorm[0].normal.x =  0.0;
ptnorm[0].normal.y =  0.0;
ptnorm[0].normal.z = -1.0;
ptnorm[1].normal.x =  0.0;
ptnorm[1].normal.y =  0.0;
ptnorm[1].normal.z = -1.0;
ptnorm[2].normal.x =  0.0;
ptnorm[2].normal.y =  0.0;
ptnorm[2].normal.z = -1.0;
ptnorm[3].normal.x =  0.0;
ptnorm[3].normal.y =  0.0;
ptnorm[3].normal.z = -1.0;
```

```
ptnorm[4].normal.x =   0.0;
ptnorm[4].normal.y =   0.0;
ptnorm[4].normal.z =  -1.0;

/* Determine and save the fill area normals */
geonorm.x = ptnorm[0].normal.x;
geonorm.y = ptnorm[0].normal.y;
geonorm.z = ptnorm[0].normal.z;
fadata.gnormal = geonorm;

/* Put the coordinate and color values into a
 * data structure */
vdata.ptconorm = ptnorm;

/* Output side 3 */
pfillarea3data (PFA_NORMAL, PVERT_COLOURNORMAL,
    PCM_RGB, &fadata, 5, &vdata);

/* Initialize side 4 vertices */
ptnorm[0].point.x = -0.1;
ptnorm[0].point.y = -0.1;
ptnorm[0].point.z = -0.1;
ptnorm[1].point.x = -0.1;
ptnorm[1].point.y = -0.1;
ptnorm[1].point.z =  0.1;
ptnorm[2].point.x = -0.1;
ptnorm[2].point.y =  0.1;
ptnorm[2].point.z =  0.1;
ptnorm[3].point.x = -0.1;
ptnorm[3].point.y =  0.1;
ptnorm[3].point.z = -0.1;
ptnorm[0].normal.x = -1.0;
ptnorm[0].normal.y =  0.0;
ptnorm[0].normal.z =  0.0;
ptnorm[1].normal.x = -1.0;
ptnorm[1].normal.y =  0.0;
ptnorm[1].normal.z =  0.0;
ptnorm[2].normal.x = -1.0;
ptnorm[2].normal.y =  0.0;
ptnorm[2].normal.z =  0.0;
ptnorm[3].normal.x = -1.0;
ptnorm[3].normal.y =  0.0;
ptnorm[3].normal.z =  0.0;
```

```
/* Determine and save the fill area normals */
geonorm.x = ptnorm[0].normal.x;
geonorm.y = ptnorm[0].normal.y;
geonorm.z = ptnorm[0].normal.z;
fadata.gnormal = geonorm;

/* Put the coordinate and color values into a
 * data structure */
vdata.ptconorm = ptnorm;

/* Output side 4 */
pfillarea3data (PFA_NORMAL, PVERT_COLOURNORMAL,
    PCM_RGB, &fadata, 4, &vdata);

/* Initialize side 5 vertices */
ptnorm[0].point.x = -0.1;
ptnorm[0].point.y =  0.1;
ptnorm[0].point.z =  0.1;
ptnorm[1].point.x =  0.0;
ptnorm[1].point.y =  0.1;
ptnorm[1].point.z =  0.1;
ptnorm[2].point.x =  0.0;
ptnorm[2].point.y =  0.1;
ptnorm[2].point.z = -0.1;
ptnorm[3].point.x = -0.1;
ptnorm[3].point.y =  0.1;
ptnorm[3].point.z = -0.1;
ptnorm[0].normal.x =  0.0;
ptnorm[0].normal.y =  1.0;
ptnorm[0].normal.z =  0.0;
ptnorm[1].normal.x =  0.0;
ptnorm[1].normal.y =  1.0;
ptnorm[1].normal.z =  0.0;
ptnorm[2].normal.x =  0.0;
ptnorm[2].normal.y =  1.0;
ptnorm[2].normal.z =  0.0;
ptnorm[3].normal.x =  0.0;
ptnorm[3].normal.y =  1.0;
ptnorm[3].normal.z =  0.0;

/* Determine and save the fill area normals */
geonorm.x = ptnorm[0].normal.x;
geonorm.y = ptnorm[0].normal.y;
geonorm.z = ptnorm[0].normal.z;
fadata.gnormal = geonorm;
```

```
/* Put the coordinate and color values into a
 * data structure */
vdata.ptconorm = ptnorm;

/* Output side 5 */
pfillarea3data (PFA_NORMAL, PVERT_COLOURNORMAL,
    PCM_RGB, &fadata, 4, &vdata);

/* Initialize side 6 vertices */
ptnorm[0].point.x = -0.1;
ptnorm[0].point.y = -0.1;
ptnorm[0].point.z =  0.1;
ptnorm[1].point.x =  0.1;
ptnorm[1].point.y = -0.1;
ptnorm[1].point.z =  0.1;
ptnorm[2].point.x =  0.1;
ptnorm[2].point.y = -0.1;
ptnorm[2].point.z = -0.1;
ptnorm[3].point.x = -0.1;
ptnorm[3].point.y = -0.1;
ptnorm[3].point.z = -0.1;
ptnorm[0].normal.x =  0.0;
ptnorm[0].normal.y = -1.0;
ptnorm[0].normal.z =  0.0;
ptnorm[1].normal.x =  0.0;
ptnorm[1].normal.y = -1.0;
ptnorm[1].normal.z =  0.0;
ptnorm[2].normal.x =  0.0;
ptnorm[2].normal.y = -1.0;
ptnorm[2].normal.z =  0.0;
ptnorm[3].normal.x =  0.0;
ptnorm[3].normal.y = -1.0;
ptnorm[3].normal.z =  0.0;

/* Determine and save the fill area normals */
geonorm.x = ptnorm[0].normal.x;
geonorm.y = ptnorm[0].normal.y;
geonorm.z = ptnorm[0].normal.z;
fadata.gnormal = geonorm;

/* Put the coordinate and color values into a
 * data structure */
vdata.ptconorm = ptnorm;
```

```
/* Output side 6 */
pfillarea3data (PFA_NORMAL, PVERT_COLOURNORMAL,
    PCM_RGB, &fadata, 4, &vdata);

/* Initialize side 7 vertices */
ptnorm[0].point.x =   0.0;
ptnorm[0].point.y =   0.1;
ptnorm[0].point.z =   0.1;
ptnorm[1].point.x =   0.1;
ptnorm[1].point.y =   0.0;
ptnorm[1].point.z =   0.1;
ptnorm[2].point.x =   0.1;
ptnorm[2].point.y =   0.0;
ptnorm[2].point.z =  -0.1;
ptnorm[3].point.x =   0.0;
ptnorm[3].point.y =   0.1;
ptnorm[3].point.z =  -0.1;
ptnorm[0].normal.x =   1.0;
ptnorm[0].normal.y =   1.0;
ptnorm[0].normal.z =   0.0;
ptnorm[1].normal.x =   1.0;
ptnorm[1].normal.y =   1.0;
ptnorm[1].normal.z =   0.0;
ptnorm[2].normal.x =   1.0;
ptnorm[2].normal.y =   1.0;
ptnorm[2].normal.z =   0.0;
ptnorm[3].normal.x =   1.0;
ptnorm[3].normal.y =   1.0;
ptnorm[3].normal.z =   0.0;

/* Determine and save the fill area normals */
geonorm.x = ptnorm[0].normal.x;
geonorm.y = ptnorm[0].normal.y;
geonorm.z = ptnorm[0].normal.z;
fadata.gnormal = geonorm;

/* Put the coordinate and color values into a
 * data structure */
vdata.ptconorm = ptnorm;

/* Output side 7 */
pfillarea3data (PFA_NORMAL, PVERT_COLOURNORMAL,
    PCM_RGB, &fadata, 4, &vdata);

}
```

```c
define_lighting(ws_id)
int ws_id;
{
#include <phigs.h>

#define LT_AMBIENT        1
#define LT_INFINITE       2
#define LT_POINT          3
#define LT_SPOT           4
#define PI                3.1415926

   Plightsrcrec        light;
   Pintlst             on_list, off_list;
   Pint                active[4];
   static Pint         inactive[1] = 0;

   /* ambient light source */
   light.ambient.colour.colour.x =  1.0;
   light.ambient.colour.colour.y =  1.0;
   light.ambient.colour.colour.z =  1.0;
   /* define ambient light source rep entry in
    *   ws_id light source table */
   psetlightsrcrep
     (ws_id, LT_AMBIENT, PLT_AMBIENT, &light);

   /* infinite light source */
   light.infinite.colour.colour.x =  1.0;
   light.infinite.colour.colour.y =  1.0;
   light.infinite.colour.colour.z =  1.0;
   light.infinite.direction.x     =  0.0;
   light.infinite.direction.y     = -1.0;
   light.infinite.direction.z     =  0.0;
   /* define infinite light source rep entry in
    * ws_id light source table */
   psetlightsrcrep
     (ws_id,LT_INFINITE,PLT_INFINITE, &light);

   /* point light source */
   light.point.position.x      =   0.0;
   light.point.position.y      =  10.0;
   light.point.position.z      =   0.0;
   light.point.colour.colour.x =   1.0;
   light.point.colour.colour.y =   1.0;
   light.point.colour.colour.z =   1.0;
   light.point.attenuation[0]  =   0.0;
```

```
light.point.attenuation[1]  =   0.0;
light.point.attenuation[2]  =   0.0;
/* define infinite light source rep entry in
 * ws_id light source table */
psetlightsrcrep
  (ws_id, LT_POINT, PLT_POINT, &light);

/* spot light source */
light.spot.colour.colour.x =   1.0;
light.spot.colour.colour.y =   1.0;
light.spot.colour.colour.z =   1.0;
light.spot.position.x       =   0.0;
light.spot.position.y       =  10.0;
light.spot.position.z       =   0.0;
light.spot.direction.x      =   0.0;
light.spot.direction.y      =  -1.0;
light.spot.direction.z      =   0.0;
light.spot.attenuation[0]   =   0.0;
light.spot.attenuation[1]   =   0.0;
light.spot.attenuation[2]   =   0.0;
light.spot.exponent         =   5.0;
light.spot.angle            =  PI/6.;
/* define infinite light source rep entry in
 * ws_id light source table */
psetlightsrcrep
  (ws_id, LT_SPOT, PLT_SPOT, &light);

/* make a list of all active light source types */
active[0] = LT_AMBIENT;
active[1] = LT_INFINITE;
active[2] = LT_POINT;
active[3] = LT_SPOT;

/* build the state list of active/inactive
 * light sources */
on_list.number    = 4;
on_list.integers  = active;
off_list.number   = 0;
off_list.integers = inactive;

/* create a structure element to set light
 *   source states */
psetlightsrcst(&on_list, &off_list);
}
```

5.3 Color Ramps

In the previous section, we performed smooth-shading with true-color workstations. In this section, we will discuss how to perform shading using a pseudo-color workstation. As we discussed in Chapter 4, often a workstation is limited to pseudo color because of the limitations of the hardware. In order to perform shading in this limited environment we must build a *color ramp*. A color ramp contains the range of colors to be used to create a smooth-shaded appearance. To understand this, let's compare the use of color ramps with what we have been doing in 5.1 and 5.2.

In Figure 5.4 we compare color tables created using set color representation (true color) and set color approximation representation (pseudo color). Refer to Chapter 4 for more detailed information concerning color tables. Table 1 in Figure 5.4 represents a color table for the true-color workstation. If a surface is created with the color index of 2, the surface will be red. When we smooth shade that surface, PHIGS will provide the different shades of red across the surface. The same is not true with pseudo color.

If we define entry 2 in the color approximation table as red, the object will be a constant shade of red. In order to create a smooth-shade of red, we must build a color ramp for entry number 2. A color ramp will use entry number 2 as the starting point for the ramp. In Table 2 of Figure 5.4, we have defined color approximation index 2 to contains five shades of red. To do this using the color approximation table, color approximation index 2 and its associated shades will

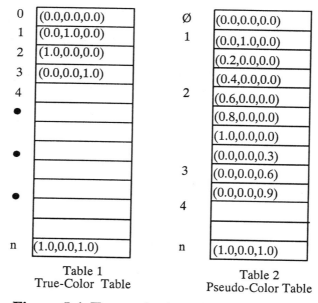

Figure 5.4. True-color/pseudo-color tables.

occupy entries 2 through 6 of the pseudo-color table. We have also defined color approximation index 3 to contain three shades of blue. Similarly, color approximation index 3 and its associated shades will occupy entries 7 through 9 of the pseudo-color table. As we can see from this example, each shade of the color index occupies an entry in the table.

The summation of the entries required for each color approximation index is limited to the maximum number of entries for the pseudo-color table. In a pseudo-color table with 256 entries, we could have a background color and 255 shades of a color or a background color and 200 shades of one color and 55 shades of another. Check your implementation for limitations on the number of shades allowed.

In both the true-color table and the pseudo-color table we have left the default background and foreground colors to be single entries. We have done this to allow us to draw a polyline using a single color without shading when using pseudo color.

Programming Example 5.3

Programming Example 5.3 is similar to Programming Example 5.2 with the addition of the subroutine define_colour_ramp and two calls to the PHIGS function psetcolourapproxindex. The same shaded object is used in both examples.

In the subroutine define_colour_ramp, we must first reinitialize the background color to contain a single entry of the color black. We then define foreground color (index 1) to be a single shade of green. Index 2 begins the first color ramp with 100 shades of red, from low to full intensity. The data element rep.record.pseudo.range in rep, which is a structure of type Pcoapproxbundl, specifies the number of shades for an index.

In Programming Example 5.3, we have created a linear ramp containing 100 shades of red. The increment between each shade, entry in the ramp, is the same, 0.075. This is an arbitrary increment. It is often useful to define a ramp using exponential, logarithmic, or trigometric functions to define an increment that is nonlinear.

The remainder of the example continues to perform the same animations as in Programming Example 5.2. This example uses no new function calls. Refer to previous sections for detailed descriptions of each of these functions.

```
/*
 *                              Example 5.3
 */
#include <phigs.h>

#define WS_ID        1
#define STRUCT_ID    1
```

```
#define VIEW_ID          1
#define CHILD_ID         2
#define LABEL            1

main()
{
    Pint          i;
    Ppoint3       pt;
    Pvector3      shift;
    Pvector3      scale;
    Pfloat        angle;
    Pmatrix3      matrix;
    Pint          error;

    /* Initialize rotation setting */
    angle = 0.0;

    /* Initialize center of object, shift vector
     * and scale */
    pt.x    = 0.0;
    pt.y    = 0.0;
    pt.z    = 0.0;
    shift.x = 0.0;
    shift.y = 0.0;
    shift.z = 0.0;
    scale.x = 1.0;
    scale.y = 1.0;
    scale.z = 1.0;

    /* Open PHIGS */
    popenphigs ("/dev/tty", 0);

    /* Open a pseudo-color double buffered
     * workstation */
    popenws (WS_ID, 0, PWST_OUTPUT_PSEUDO_DB);

    /* Define a view for the workstation */
    define_angle_view (WS_ID, VIEW_ID);

    /* Define a color ramp */
    define_colour_ramp (WS_ID);

    /* Set HLHSR mode =This turns on z-buffering for
     * the workstation */
    psethlhsrmode (WS_ID, 1);
```

```
/* Open a parent structure */
popenstruct (STRUCT_ID);

/* Set HLHSR ID This turns on Z-buffering for
 * this structure */
psethlhsrid (1);

/* Set the view index */
psetviewind (VIEW_ID);

/* Set color approximation index */
psetcolouraproxind (1);

/* Create an axis */
create_axis ();

/* Set a label This serves as a pointer to the
 * following structure element */
plabel (LABEL);

/* Initialize matrix to identity (normal) - No
 * structure element is created, just a matrix
 * in main memory */
identity3 (matrix);

/* Set the identity matrix as the local
 * transformation matrix A structure element is
 * created. The label is therefore just before
 * this structure element.  Later we will come
 * back to edit this structure element
 * containing the set local transform element */
psetlocaltran3 (matrix, PREPLACE);

/* Execute the child structure - The child
 * structure will be created later.  Nothing
 * will be executed until the structure network
 * is traversed (using predrawallstruct or
 * pupdatews).  We cannot create child structure
 * now because we already have a structure Open.
 * When executed, the child structure will
 * inherit the above transformation and view
 * from the parent. */
pexecutestruct (CHILD_ID);
```

```
/* Close the structure */
pclosestruct ();

/* Open the child structure */
popenstruct (STRUCT_ID);

/* Define surface characteristics */
define_surface (1, 4, PSH_COLOUR, PSOLID);

/* Define light sources */
define_lighting (WS_ID);

/* Set color approximation index */
psetcolouraproxind (1);

/* Draw the object */
create_lighted_object ();

/* Close the child structure */
pclosestruct ();

/* Post the parent structure to the workstation
 * Note: only the parent structure is posted.
 * The child structure will be executed by the
 * parent. */
ppoststruct (WS_ID, STRUCT_ID, 0.0);

/* Redraw all structures posted to the
 * workstation */
predrawallstruct (WS_ID, PALWAYS);

/* Set edit mode to replace - This will put all
 * succeding calls into the same place in DLM so
 * that just the one Set local  transformation
 * instruction will be changed (Note: a common
 * mistake is to forget to reset edit mode to
 * INSERT before defining a new structure,
 * resulting in a structure which contains
 * nothing) */
pseteditmode (PEDIT_REPLACE);

/* Open parent structure so it can be edited */
popenstruct (STRUCT_ID);
```

```
/* Set the element pointer to the beginning of
 * the parent  structure the pointer will be at
 * the end of the structure if  you don't reset
 * it to the beginning */
psetelemptr (0);

/* Set the element pointer to the label - This
 * points to the label, to replace the local
 * matrix the pointer will have to  be offset to
 * the ext element in the structure */
psetelemptrlabel (LABEL);

/* Offset the element pointer to point to the
 * local  transformation */
poffsetelemptr (1);

/* Now we are pointing to the Set local
 * transform structure  element in the structure
 * network.  We'll loop, changing the
 * translation vector each loop to move the
 * object around the  origin in a circular
 * fashion.  A translation matrix is  created
 * which replaces the previous local marix in
 * the  structure network.  The structure
 * network is re-traversed to show the object
 * in it's new position */

/* Do for a while */
for (i=0; i<100; i++)
  {
  /* Increment rotation values */
  angle = angle + 0.1;

  /* Build transformation matrix */
  pbuildtran3 (&pt, &shift, angle, angle, angle,
               &scale, &error, matrix);

   /* Set the local transformation matrix - This is
    * the structure element to be replaced */
   psetlocaltran3 (matrix, PPRECONCATENATE);

   /* Redraw all structures - This will redraw all
    * structures posted to the workstation */
   predrawallstruct (WS_ID, PALWAYS);
```

```
      /* Sleep */
      sleep (1);
   }
/* End do */

/* Close the structure that was Open for editing
 * This is often forgotten, creating a state
 * error when trying to Open another structure*/
pclosestruct ();

/* Set edit mode to insert - Although this it
 * not necessary in this example (as no more
 * structure creation will take place), it is a
 * good idea to get into the habit of always re-
 * setting the edit mode to insert (the
 * default).  Forgetting to do so will cause
 * problems later in more complex programs.  You
 * will be in a situation where every structure
 * element is overwritten, creating structures
 * containing nothing */
pseteditmode (PEDIT_INSERT);

/* Close the workstation */
pclosews (WS_ID);

/* Close PHIGS */
pclosephigs ();
}



define_colour_ramp (ws_id)
int    ws_id;
{
#include <phigs.h>

#define BACKGROUND    0
              /* Background color approx index */
#define FOREGROUND    1
              /* Foreground color approx index */
#define RAMP_INDEX    2
              /* Ramp color approx index       */
#define TBL_SIZE      100
              /* # of shades in ramp           */
```

```
Pint          i;                        /* Loop counter */
Pfloat        colour_val;
                        /* Incremental color value */
Pfloat        colour_inc;
                        /* Loop color increment */
Pcoapproxbundl rep;
                /* Color approximation structure */
Pcobundl      ramp_table[TBL_SIZE];
                            /* Ramp color values */
Pcobundl      table[1];
                /* Fore/Background color values */

/* You must first reset the background to have only
 * one color. This makes room in the color lookup
 * table to build the ramp */

/* Assign constants to color approx representation
 * data structure */
rep.method                = PPSEUDO;
                        /* psuedo (8-bit) color */
rep.record.pseudo.range   = 1;
                        /* # entries in table    */
rep.record.pseudo.weight[0] = 0.33;
                        /*      We'll give RGB    */
rep.record.pseudo.weight[1] = 0.33;
                        /*       equal weight     */
rep.record.pseudo.weight[2] = 0.33;
                        /*         for now.       */
rep.record.pseudo.model   = PCM_RGB;
                        /*         use RGB        */

/* Assign red, green and blue values -
 * All zero yields black */
table[0].x = 0.0;
table[0].y = 0.0;
table[0].z = 0.0;

/* Assign RGB values to color approx
 * representation data  structure */
rep.record.pseudo.colours = table;

/* Set color approximation representation for the
 * background index */
psetcolourapproxrep (ws_id, BACKGROUND, &rep);
```

```
/* Assign red, green and blue values */
table[0].x = 0.0;
table[0].y = 1.0;
table[0].z = 0.0;

/* Assign RGB values to color approx
 * representation  data structure */
rep.record.pseudo.colours = table;

/* Set color approximation representation for the
 * foreground index */
psetcolourapproxrep (ws_id, FOREGROUND, &rep);

/* Build a color ramp with TBL_SIZE increments
 * between full intensity and black. The ramp values
 * will be stored in the  red component of the color
 * triplet with no color component of either green
 * or blue. * /

/* Initialize color table increment and
 * intensity*/
colour_inc = (0.75 / (float) TBL_SIZE);
colour_val = 0.25;

/* Do for each ramp shade */
for (i = 0; i < TBL_SIZE; i++)
    {
    /* Set RED color component to the current
     * intensity. This creates the different
     * shades*/
    ramp_table[i].x = colour_val;

    /* Set GREEN and BLUE color components to
     * zero or they could be set to any other
     * value between 0.0 and 1.0 either together
     * or seperately */
    ramp_table[i].y = 0.0;
    ramp_table[i].z = 0.0;

    /* Decrement the intensity */
        colour_val = colour_val + colour_inc;
    }
/* End do for each ramp shade */
```

```
/* Set the table size.  It was set to 1 to reset
 * the background. Everything else stays the
 * same.*/
rep.record.pseudo.range = TBL_SIZE;

/* Assign look up table to the color structure */
rep.record.pseudo.colours = ramp_table;

/* Set the color approximation representation for
 * the ramp shade */
psetcolourapproxrep (ws_id, RAMP_INDEX, &rep);
}
```

Review Questions

1. What is a color ramp?

2. Modify Programming Example 5.1 to draw the color cube presented at the end of Chapter 4.

3. How is Gouraud shading performed?

4. List applications where Gouraud shading can be useful.

5. Modify the increments in the color ramp presented in Programming Example 5.3.

6. What are the different types of light reflected by the surface of an object?

7. Modify the ratios of the light reflected by the object in Programming Example 5.2. Observe the difference in the appearance of the object.

8. What are the different types of light sources?

9. Modify Programming Example 5.2 to turn off and on the light source combinations presented in the example.

10. Modify Programming Example 5.3 to use a non-linear color ramp. Observe the difference in the displayed object.

11. Use geometric normals to produce the smooth-shaded object presented in this chapter.

6
PHIGS Input Devices

Introduction

All of the example images presented up to this point have been modified via program control. PHIGS, however, provides the application programmer with a variety of *logical input device* types that allow the user to interact with the display. A logical input device is an abstraction of one or more physical devices that provides input to the PHIGS program. A mouse, for example, is one physical device. As we shall see in Section 2.2, however, the buttons on the mouse are seen as separate, independent input devices. Each mouse button is said to be a logical input device. In this chapter we discuss the different types of devices allowed by PHIGS. On completion of this chapter, the reader will be able to initialize and read a logical input device.

The INPUT and OUTIN workstation types can have one or more input devices. When one of these workstation types is opened, a workstation description table is created that includes a list of all available input devices. The default values of this list are modified when an input device is initialized by the application program.

Within PHIGS there are six different types of logical input devices; *choice, locator, string, pick, stroke,* and *valuator*. Table 6.1 presents a description of the six different types of input devices. The class within which a device falls is determined by the characteristics of the input device and how it is used by the PHIGS program. A mouse can be used as a pick device that is used to select items from the screen or a mouse can be used as stroke device to input a sequence of points.

A logical input device is controlled by four processes; an *echo process,* a *measure process,* a *trigger process,* and an *acknowledgment process.* Each process handles a separate phase of the overall input process. The measure process contains the current state of the input device. If the input device is a valuator, for example, the position of that valuator will be held by the measure process. We will discuss valuator input devices in more detail in Section 6.1. When a significant event occurs the trigger process is said to have *fired.* The firing of a trigger process sends a message to one or more logical input devices.

Table 6.1. Input device types.

Device type	Description
Choice	Returns an integer ≥ 0 which identifies a selection alternative
Locator	Returns a world coordinate and a view index
String	Returns a character string
Pick	Returns the "Path Name" which identifies a structure element that was chosen from the screen
Stroke	Returns a stream of world coordinates
Valuator	Returns a real number

When the trigger process is fired, the acknowledge process sends to the operator some sort of feedback to indicate the trigger process. The echo process provides output that indicates the current value of the logical input device, such as the cursor for a locator input device or a small box on a slide bar for a valuator device.

An input device can be opened in one of three modes; *request, sample,* and *event.* The mode determines when data are received from the input device. In request mode, data are read from the input device when requested by the application program. When the request function is called, the device prompt is displayed and the application program waits for a response from the input device. The logical input devices are normally set to request mode as part of the default. Reading from a standard alphanumeric terminal is an example of request mode. The user is prompted for input and the program suspends until a response is read.

In sample mode, the value of the input device when it is read by the application program is the value that is passed back to the application program. If the value of the input device changes after it is sampled, and then changes back to the original value before it is sampled again, the change in values will not be detected by the PHIGS program. Let us say, for example, that we are sampling the movement of a mouse to position a cursor on a screen. We first sample the mouse as moving two units to the left, we then go and move the cursor on the screen two units left. If while we are moving the cursor, the user moves the mouse up two units and then back down two units to the original position, the cursor will remain stationary on the screen.

In event mode, the input device creates an event that is queued by PHIGS and read by the PHIGS program. An activity on an input device will create an event, such as the clicking of a mouse button or the typing of a key. Events are stored in a queue and read by the PHIGS program by the *AWAIT EVENT* function. The await event function returns to the application program the input device that generated the event. The PHIGS program can then read the value of the input device with the get function. PHIGS also provides a *FLUSH DEVICE EVENTS* to flush the event queue. A mouse button that is read in event mode by the PHIGS program will generate an event each time the button is pushed. The PHIGS program can then read the event queue and respond to the mouse button. If the user pushes the mouse button many times, the PHIGS program can respond to simply the first button push and flush the queue of the rest.

Each of the six input devices is initialized and read in a similar manner. The following sections of this chapter will demonstrates the use of two of these input devices types. Section 6.1 will demonstrate the use of a valuator input device. Section 2 describes the use of a locator device. The remaining types of input devices are left for the reader's experimentation.

6.1 Valuator Input Device

A valuator device is a logical input device providing a real number. The example in this chapter will use a knob box as its valuator device. The real number returned by the valuator device for the knob box is a function of the angle of the position of the dial. A valuator device can be any logical device. A mouse, for example, that uses a slide bar as a form of input is a valuator device. The valuator returns for the slide bar the position of the mouse on the slide bar.

The data, for example, can then be used to scale a feature of the display. A common use of a knob box is to rotate a structure. If, for example, we use a knob to represent the rotation of a structure around the Z axis, the degree to which the dial is turned tells the program how many degrees to rotate the structure. If the dial is turned 10°, the PHIGS program can then rotate the structure 10°. A slide bar can represent depth of color, as the slide bar is moved the PHIGS program can change the intensity of the colors in the color lookup table for that workstation.

The manner in which the application program takes advantage of the versatility of a valuator device is dependent on creativity of the PHIGS programmer. In the following example, we present the initialization and reading of a valuator device. The reader can incorporate these subroutines into their own application.

Programming Example 6.1

Programming Example 6.1 consists of two subroutines that may be called by a PHIGS program. The first subroutine, init_valuator, initializes a valuator device, a knob box. The subroutine sets the initial values of the knob box data structures and sets the valuator input mode to sample. The program then enters a loop to read the valuator device. At the top of the loop the program calls the user subroutine get_valuator, which reads input from a valuator device. The program checks to see which knob on the valuator device was turned and prints a message reporting the input.

Initializing a Valuator Input Device

Prior to use, a valuator input device must be initialized by the PHIGS program. The following PHIGS function call initializes a valuator input device:

```
pinitval
  (ws_id, dev, init, pet, &echo_area, &record);
                  /* (PHOP,WSOP, *,*)*/
```

In the example program, this function is called for each of the dials on the knob box. When the function is executed, the initial value, prompt/echo type, echo volume and valuator data record are stored in the workstation state list for each valuator device. In the example, each knob on the knob box is a separate valuator device.

The function receives as input the id of the workstation with which the input device is to be associated, ws_id. The second input parameter, dev, is the device number of the input device that is being initialized. The third parameter, init, is the initial value of the valuator device; in the example, we have set this value to 0.0.

The function also receives as input a prompt/echo type. The PHIGS defined values for this parameter are described in Table 6.2. The prompt/echo is

Table 6.2. Prompt/echo types.

Value	Description
≤ 0	Prompting and echoing is valuator and device-dependent
1	Designate the current valuator value using an implementation defined technique
2	Display a graphical representation of the current valuator value within the echo volume
3	Display a digital representation of the current valuator value within the echo volume
≥ 4	Reserved for registration

displayed in the echo volume, which is the next parameter in the function call. The echo volume describes in device coordinates where the echo for the valuator input device is to be display on the output device.

The final input parameter to the function is a valuator record. This record contains the range of values that is acceptable from the valuator. In the example, we have used a range of -1.0 to 1.0. This range can be set to any value. For example, a range of +pi to -pi or a range of 0.0 to 100.0 may be used. For all valuator prompt/echo types, the valuator will be scaled linearly according to the specified range. The valuator record also contains a title string, which is used when a prompt is displayed. Since we have chosen not to display a prompt, this field is NULL.

Set the Valuator Input Mode

Once the subroutine has initialized the valuator input devices, the program sets the input mode of each of the dials. The following PHIGS function call sets the input mode of the valuator devices:

```
psetvalmode
        (ws_id, dev, PSAMPLE, PES_NOECHO);
                        /*(PHOP,WSOP,*,*)*/
```

In the example program, this function is called for each of the valuator input devices. When this function is executed, the valuator device identified by the input parameter dev of the workstation identified by ws_id is set to the specified operating mode.

The third input parameter, operating mode, is an enumeration type having the values PREQUEST, PSAMPLE, and PEVENT. Refer to the introduction of this chapter for a description of each of these modes. The last input to the function is the echo state. This parameter is an enumeration type with the values PES_ECHO and PES_NOECHO. The input device state defined by the operating mode and echo mode is stored in the workstation state list for the given valuator device.

Reading Valuator Input

The subroutine get_valuator reads a value from the valuator input device. If the valuator were opened in request mode, the value of the valuator would be read with the PHIGS function prequestval. The valuator in the example, however, was opened in sample mode and uses the following PHIGS function to read the value of the valuator:

```
psampleval (ws_id, dev, &valuator);
                        /*(PHOP,WSOP,*,*)*/
```

This function returns the current measure of the valuator device. The value is in the range specified in the workstation state list entry for this device in the valuator data record. This is the range that was specified when the input device was initialized.

The measure of the valuator device is the real value that represents the location of the valuator device. If this is a dial on a knob box, it is the position to which the dial has been turned. If it is a slide bar, it is where on the bar the valuator is located. The subroutine reads each of the three dials that have been initialized and stores them in the appropriate variable. When the program terminates, these values are passed back to the calling program.

```c
/*
 *                            Example 6.1
 */
#include <phigs.h>
#define WS_ID       1
main ()
{
    Pfloat knob_1, knob_2, knob_3;
                    /* value for each of 3 knobs */
    Pfloat save_1, save_2, save_3;
                    /* saved value for each knob */
    /* Open PHIGS */
    popenphigs ("/dev/tty", 0);

    /* Open a true-colour workstation as
     * input/output If you forget you'll get a
     * message saying the input device is not
     * available */
    popenws (WS_ID, 0, PWST_OUTIN_TRUE);

    /* Initialize the valuator devices */
    init_valuator (WS_ID);

    /* Initialize the temp values */
    save_1 = 0.0;
    save_2 = 0.0;
    save_3 = 0.0;

    /* Loop */
    while (1)
        {
        /* Read the valuator device */
        get_valuator
            (WS_ID, &knob_1, &knob_2, &knob_3);
        /* Check each knob. If it has moved, print and
```

```
              * save its value */
        if (save_1 != knob_1)
          {
          printf ("Knob #1 = %d\n");
          save_1 = knob_1;
          }
        if (save_2 != knob_2)
          {
          printf ("Knob #2 = %d\n");
          save_2 = knob_2;
          }
        if (save_3 != knob_3)
          {
          printf ("Knob #3 = %d\n");
          save_3 = knob_3;
          }
      }
    /* Close the workstation */
    pclosews (WS_ID);

    /* Close PHIGS */
    pclosephigs ();
}




#define NUMDEV 3
init_valuator (ws_id)
Pint ws_id;
{
Pint        i;                  /* loop counter */
Pint        dev;                /* device #, each knob
                                   is different */
Pfloat      init;               /* initial position */
Pint        pet;                /*prompt and echo type*/
Plimit      echo_area;          /* Not used        */
Pvalrec     record;             /* data structure to
                                   transfer input data*/
Pint        idev[NUMDEV];       /* device dependent
                                   device numbers */

    /*Initialize device numbers as per system
     * instructions */
    idev[0] = 3;        /*    WARNING         */
```

```
idev[1] = 4;          /*Check your system
                       *     documentation   */
idev[2] = 5;          /*for correct values. */

/* Initialize valuator values */
init = 0.0;
pet = 1;
/* Put hi/low values into knob data structure -
 * you can set these for whatever values you
 * want (ie: -pi to +pi, 0 to 100, etc). */
record.valpet1_datarec.low  = -1.0;
record.valpet1_datarec.high =  1.0;
/* Unused for knob box - Some implementations
 * use this as a label for on-screen sliders */
record.valpet1_datarec.data = "";
/* Initialize echo area */
echo_area.xmin = 0.0;
echo_area.xmax = 1.0;
echo_area.ymin = 0.0;
echo_area.ymax = 1.0;

/* Do for each knob to be used */
for(i = 0; i < NUMDEV; i++)
    {
    /* Set the device number - Note: Each knob
     * has a different device number; check your
     * PHIGS implementation */
    dev = idev[i];

    /* Initialize a knob as a valuator device
     * and the initial value as 0.0 */
    pinitval (ws_id,dev,init,pet,
                &echo_area,&record);

    /* Set the valuator input mode to event -
     * Note: Event mode generates an event
     * report in the event queue; await event
     * and get valuator are used to read event
     * reports; echo area is ignored with knob
     * box. */
    psetvalmode (ws_id, dev, PSAMPLE,
                        PES_NOECHO);
    }
/* End do for each knob to be used */
}
```

```
get_valuator (ws_id, dial_1, dial_2, dial_3)
float *dial_1;
float *dial_2;
float *dial_3;
{

    Pint   dev;
    Pfloat   valuator;
    Pfloat fvalue;

    /* Do for each device */
    for (dev = 3; dev < 6; i++)
        {
        /* Request valuator */
        psampleval (ws_id, dev, &valuator);

        if (dev == 3)  *dial_1 = valuator;
        if (dev == 4)  *dial_2 = valuator;
        if (dev == 5)  *dial_3 = valuator;
        }
}
```

6.2 Locator Device

A locator input device provides a position in world coordinates and a view index. The coordinate is the position in world coordinates that corresponds to the location selected on the display surface. The world coordinate is derived by taking the location on the display surface and reversing the transformation pipeline, which was described in Chapter 2. Basically, the coordinate swims upstream in the transformation pipeline. The view index is the view index for the workstation that is active for that point on the display surface.

A locator input device is not to be confused with a pick input device. A pick input device returns a *path* to the structure element that was selected by the pick input device. A pick input device is used to identify specific output primitives that are displayed on the workstation. The locator input device is used to identify locations in world coordinate space.

The locator input device allows the user of the PHIGS program to interact with the PHIGS application in the world coordinate space. This maps well into the real world since the world coordinate space is the coordinate system in which the objects are defined. The following programming example will demonstrates how to initialize and read a locator input device.

Programming Example 6.2

Programming Example 6.2 consist of two subroutines that may be called by a PHIGS program. As in the previous example when we initialized a valuator device, we first initialize locator devices and then set the input mode. The first subroutine, init_locator, initializes a separate locator device for each button on a mouse. The second subroutine, get_locator, reads input from a locator device.

This example also demonstrate how an input device opened in event mode is accessed. The get_locator subroutine begins by waiting on an event. Once an event occurs, the event class is checked to determine which button caused the event. Note the difference between an event input device and a sample input device. When working with sample input devices, the input is taken from the device by the process without waiting for an event to trigger the reading of the value. With an event input device, the process waits for the input to arrive.

Initializing a Locator Device

Prior to use, the locator input device must be initialized. The following PHIGS function call initializes a locator input device:

pinitloc(ws_id, 0, &init, 0, &echo_area, &record);
/*(PHOP,WSOP,*,*)*/

The first parameter to the function call is the workstation identifier, ws_id. The second parameter to the function call is the device number of the device that is to be initialized. When this function is executed, the input parameters are stored in an entry in the workstation state list for the workstation identified by ws_id.

The third parameter to the function call, init, is a structure identifying the initial locator position and the view index. The PHIGS standard does not require that these data items be bound together in a structure, although the implementation used for the examples has done so. As with all the examples presented in this text, the reader should check how their implementation expects to receive these data. The first element of this data structure is an integer value specifying the index into the workstation's view table (Chapter 2). The second element of the data structure is the initial position of the locator. The locator's position is specified in world coordinates.

The function also receives as input a prompt/echo type. The PHIGS defined values for this parameter are described in Table 6.2. The prompt/echo type defines how the locator is displayed on the screen. The function also receives as input an echo volume. The echo volume describes in device coordinates where the echo for the locator input device is to be display on the output device. In the implementation used for these examples, the value was not used, again check the documentation of this parameter to determine what your implementation expects.

Setting the Input Mode

After the locator has been initialized, the example program tells PHIGS how it wants to receive the data from the input device. The following PHIGS function call sets the input mode for the locator input device:

```
psetlocmode(ws_id, 1, PEVENT, PES_ECHO);
                    /*(PHOP,WSOP.*,*,)*/
```

The function receives as input the identifier of the workstation with which the input device is associated. The second parameter is the device number of the locator input device. The third input parameter, operating mode, is an enumeration type having the values PREQUEST, PSAMPLE, and PEVENT. Refer to the introduction of this chapter for a description of each of these modes. The echo state of the locator device is an enumeration type with the values PES_ECHO and PES_NOECHO. The input device state defined by the operating mode and echo mode is stored in the workstation state list for the given locator device.

Waiting for an Event

The example program calls the subroutine get_locator to read the locator device. Since the device has been opened in event mode, we must check to see if an event has occurred before we can read the device. The following PHIGS function call waits on an event:

```
pawaitevent(timeout, &event);
                    /*(PHOP,WSOP,*,*)*/
```

The function receives as input a timeout period which is the maximum time period that PHIGS should wait on the event. If the input queue is empty, PHIGS is placed in a wait state until an input event is placed in the queue and the wait time has exceeded what has been specified by the timeout input parameter. If a timeout occurs and there is still no entry in the queue, a NONE value is returned for the input class. If there is at least one entry in the queue, the oldest event report is moved from the event queue to the *current event report* in the PHIGS state list.

The function returns workstation identifier, the input class, and the logical input device number. The input class is an enumeration type having the values: NONE, LOCATOR, STROKE, VALUATOR, CHOICE, PICK, and STRING. These values are then used latter as input to the get function that reads the event report.

Getting an Event Report

Once control is returned from the PHIGS function, the subroutine checks to see if there was an event and if that event was the locator device. The program reads event reports for the locator device with the following PHIGS function:

```
    pgetloc (&locator);    /*(PHOP,WSOP, *,*)*/
```

The function returns the locator position in world coordinates and the view index. The view index is an index to the workstation's view table. The view pointed at by this index is the view that was used in the conversion from a coordinate on the surface of the display device to a world coordinate.

```
/*
 *                         Example 6.2
 */
#include <phigs.h>

#define WS_ID      1

main ()
{

    /* Open PHIGS */
    popenphigs ("/dev/tty", 0);

    /* Open a true-colour workstation as
     * input/output - If you forget you'll get a
     * message saying the input device is not
     * available */
    popenws (WS_ID, 0, PWST_OUTIN_TRUE);

    /* Initialize the locator devices */
    init_locator (WS_ID);

    /* Read the locator device */
    get_locator ();

    /* Close the workstation */
    pclosews (WS_ID);

    /* Close PHIGS */
    pclosephigs ();
}


init_locator(ws_id)
int    ws_id;
{
    Ploc    init;
    Plocrec record;
```

```
    Plimit   echo_area;
    int             i;

    /* Initialize echo area */
    echo_area.xmin = 0.0;
    echo_area.xmax = 1.0;
    echo_area.ymin = 0.0;
    echo_area.ymax = 1.0;

    /* Initialize initial location */
    init.position.x = 0.5;
    init.position.y = 0.5;

    /* Initialize the data record */
    record.locpet1_datarec.data = 0;

    /* Initialize the locator devices - Each mouse
     * button is a different device.  Check
     * implementation for device numbers. */
    pinitloc (ws_id, 0, &init, 1,
                       &echo_area, &record);
    pinitloc(ws_id, 1, &init, 1, &echo_area,
                                  &record);
    pinitloc(ws_id, 2, &init, 1, &echo_area,
                                  &record);

    /* Set event mode */
    psetlocmode(ws_id, 0, PEVENT, PES_ECHO);
    psetlocmode(ws_id, 1, PEVENT, PES_ECHO);
    psetlocmode(ws_id, 2, PEVENT, PES_ECHO);
}


get_locator ()
{
Pfloat       timeout = {2.0};   /*time of wait for
                                              event*/
Pevent       event;
Ploc   locator;

    while(1)
      {
      /* Wait specified time for an event */
      pawaitevent(timeout, &event);
```

```
      /* If there was an event then */
      if (event.class != PI_NONE)
        {
        /* If the event was from a locator device
         * then */
        if (event.class == PI_LOCATOR)
          {
          /* Get the locator data */
          pgetloc (&locator);

          /* If this is the first mouse button
           * then*/
          if (event.dev == 0)

            /* Print the X-location */
            printf  ("X Location = %f\n",
                                  locator.position.x);

          /* Else if this is the second mouse button
           * then */
          else if (event.dev == 1)

            /* Print the Y-location */
            printf ("Y Location = %f\n",
                                  locator.position.y);

          /* Else if this is the third mouse button
           * then */
          else if (event.dev == 2)

            /* Print the view index */
            printf ("View Index = %d\n",
                                  locator.view_index);

          /*End if this is the first mouse button */
          }
        /* End if the event was from a locator
         * device*/
        }
      /* End if there was an event */
      }
    /* End do while */
  }
```

Review Questions

1. What workstation types receive input?

2. What is a logical input device? Does a logical input device differ from an input device?

3. How is a logical input device controlled?

4. What are the different types of logical input device?

5. What are the different types of input mode?

6. Change the input mode of both examples to REQUEST. Observe the difference in how they interact with the user.

7. Using Programming Example 6.1 as a starting point. Write a PHIGS program that reads a valuator device and uses the returned values to rotate the object presented in Chapter 5.

8. Using Programming Example 6.2 as a starting point. Write a PHIGS program that reads a locator device and translates the object displayed in Chapter 5 to the input location.

9. Write a PHIGS program that reads a PICK device initialized to event mode. Have the PHIGS program display the object presented in Chapter 5. When the PICK device identifies a side of the object allow a valuator device change the intensity of that side's color.

Appendix A
Packing FORTRAN Records

```
      subroutine pacrec (wkid)
c
c     This is the Fortran version of define_colour_ramp.c
c     Its purpose is to demonstrate the PHIGS Fortran routine
c     PPREC.  The C language has the ability to put
c     characters, reals, and integers into the same data
c     structure, Fortran does not.  PPREC is a PHIGS
c     Fortran function which takes as input integers,
c     reals, and character strings and converts them to
c     be fully contained in a single character string, the
c     record.  The PSCAR PHIGS Fortran routine expects a
c     record packed as follows:
c        il:  length of array ia (in this case 2)
c        ia:  array containing the range and color model
c        rl:length of array rl ([3 + (3 X range)]. This is 3
c     values for the weight and 3 values for each shade in
c     the ramp)
c        ra:  array containing weights and colors
c        sl:  number of character strings (in this case 0)
c        lstr: lengths of each character string (in this case 0)
c        str: strings (in this case null)
c
c     Note: Fortran uses a different enumeration file than C
      include '/usr/include/phigsf77.h'

      parameter (idback = 0, idfore = 1, idramp = 2)
      parameter (irange = 100)

c.....You must estimate the size of the data record to
c       bepacked doesn't hurt of over-estimate.  The size is the
c       number of characters PPREC will pack into the data
```

```
c     record.  A string containing an integer with value 1, a
c     real with value 2.2, and a string 'String' would look
c     like:
c
c     12.2String
c
c     As each record is 80 characters, the above string would
c     easily fit into 1 record.  If there were 81 characters
c     you would need 2 records.  For the ramp we will need 2
c     characters for the integers (ia(1) and ia(2)) and XXX
c     for each shade in the ramp.

      integer    wkid,
      +          i,
      +          ldr
      integer    il,
      +          ia(2),
      +          sl,
      +          lstr(1),
      +          mldr,
      +          rl
      real   ra(3+(irange*3))
      real   rval,
      +              colour_inc
      character*1 str(1)
      character*80      record(99)

c.....You must first reset the background to have only one
c     color.  This makes room in the color lookup table to
c     build the ramp.  Assign constants to color approx
c     representation data record

      il    = 2
      ia(1) = 1
      ia(2) = PRGB
      rl    = 3 + (ia(1)*3)
      ra(1) = 0.33
      ra(2) = 0.33
      ra(3) = 0.33
      sl    = 0
      lstr(1)    = 0
      str(1)     = '0'
      mldr  = 99

c.....Assign red, green and blue values for the background
```

```
c      color

       ra(4) = 0.0
       ra(5) = 0.0
       ra(6) = 0.0

c.....Pack the data record for the background color

       write (*,*) 'packing background'
       call pprec (il, ia, rl, ra, sl, lstr, str, mldr,
     +       errind, ldr, record)
       write (*,*) record

c.....Set the color approximation for the background with
c.....data packed into the record

       call pscar (wkid, idback, PRGB, record)

c.....Assign red, green and blue values for the foreground
c      color

       ra(4) = 0.0
       ra(5) = 1.0
       ra(6) = 0.0

c.....Pack the data record for the foreground color

       call pprec (il, ia, rl, ra, sl, lstr, str, mldr,
     +       errind, ldr, record)
       write (*,*) record

c.....Set the color approximation for the foreground with
c      data packed into the record

       call pscar (wkid, idfore, PRGB, record)

c.....Build a color ramp with [irange] increments between full
c      intensity and black. The ramp values will be stored in
c      the red component of the color triplet with no color
c      component of either green or blue.

c.....Initialize color table increment and intensity

       colour_inc = 0.75 / float (irange)
       colour_val = 0.25
```

```
c.....Do for each ramp shade

      do i = 1, (irange*3), 3

c.......Set the red, green, and blue value for this shade

      ra(i) = colour_val
      ra(i+1) = 0.0
      ra(i+2) = 0.0

c.......Increment the intensity

      colour_val = colour_val + colour_inc

c.....End do for each shade

      end do

c.....Re-assign constants to colour approx representation data
c     record which change for the ramp

      ia(1) = irange
      rl    = 3 + (ia(1)*3)

c.....Pack the data record for the ramp color

      call pprec (il, ia, rl, ra, sl, lstr, str, mldr,
     +      errind, ldr, record)
      write (*,*) record

c.....Set the color approximation for the ramp with
c     data packed into the record

      call pscar (wkid, idramp, PRGB, record)

c.....Return

      return
      end
```

Glossary

A

Acknowledgment -Output to the operator of a logical input device indicating that a trigger has been fired.

Addressable point -Any point of a device that can be addressed.

Ambient light -A type of light source that enters into the lighting calculation independent of the orientation of the surface being illuminated or the location of the eye.

Ambient reflection coefficient -The fraction of ambient light being reflected from the surface.

Ancestor structure -A parent structure or the parent of a parent structure.

Annotation -A class of output primitives that is defined in normalized projection coordinates but is placed with respect to a reference point, which may be anywhere in modelling coordinate space. The plane on which the annotation appears is always parallel to the X-Y plane of the display space and is unaffected by modeling and viewing transformations, but the reference point is transformed in the normal manner.

Annotation style -An aspect of annotation that determines its representation on the display surface of all workstations.

Archive file -A mechanism for the storage and transportation of graphical data, represented by PHIGS structures and their contents.

Area defining primitive -Any primitive whose attributes may be derived from the interior representation table. In PHIGS+, fill area, fill area set, triangle strip, quadrilateral mesh, polyhedron, nonuniform B-spline surface, and parametric polynomial surface are considered to be area-defining primitives.

Aspect ratio -The ratio of lengths along the principal axes of an object.

Aspects of primitives -The appearance of primitives is controlled by the values of a set of characteristics called aspect examples of which are the height of a character or the line type of a polyline. Geometric aspects are workstation independent and are controlled by the corresponding attributes. For nongeometric aspects, the mapping between a particular aspect and its controlling attribute is defined by the associated aspect source flag (ASF). If the ASF is set to BUNDLED, this aspect of the primitive is controlled by the bundle index attribute. If the ASF is set to INDIVIDUAL, the aspect is controlled by the corresponding attribute.

Aspect source flag -A flag indicating whether a particular workstation dependent aspect of a primitive is selected from an attribute bundle or as an individual attribute selection.

Attribute -Attributes control the properties of output primitives. There are four types of attributes: geometric, nongeometric, viewing, and identification. The geometric and nongeometric attributes control the values of aspects of primitives.

B

Back action -An implementation dependent and workstation-dependent mechanism enabling the operator to interrupt an input operation.

Back face -Any portion of an area-defining primitive whose geometric normal when transformed to NPC has a negative Z component. Back-facing portions can be subjected to special attributes or made invisible.

Back plane -A plane parallel to the view plane whose location is specified as an N coordinate value in view reference coordinate system. Primitives behind the back plane lie outside the view volume.

Bundle index -An attribute of an output primitive that is an index into a bundle table. It defines the workstation dependent aspects of the primitive.

Bundle table -A workstation dependent table specifying aspects of one or more output primitives. PHIGS has polyline, polymarker, text, interior, and edge bundle tables.

Bundle table entry -A single entry is a bundle table. Each entry contains one value for each aspect that applies to the corresponding output primitive. This set is workstation dependent.

C

Cell array -An output primitive consisting of a parallelogram of equal-sized cells, each of which is a parallelogram and has a single color.

Centralized Structure Store (CSS) -The conceptual workstation-independent storage area for structure networks.

Character body -The rectangle defining the horizontal and vertical limits of an individual character.

Character expansion factor -An aspect of text that specifies the deviation of character width from the defined normal value.

Character set -A registered interpretation for entries in the character code table.

Character spacing -An aspect of text that specifies the fraction of font nominal character height to be added between ajacent character bodies in a string.

Character up vector -An aspect of text that defines the principal up direction of the text string. It is a two-dimensional vector in the text plane specified in the text structure element.

Child structure -A structure specified in a structure reference.

Choice device -A logical input device providing a non-negative integer defining one of a set of alternatives.

CIE -Commision Internationale de l'Eclairage. Used to refer to the CIE universal color definition system used as a color model.

Clipping -Removing those parts of output primitives that lie outside a specified volume.

Color approximation -The workstation-dependent function that takes colors in the rendering color model, perhaps transforms them, and displays them on the workstation as accurately as possible.

Color index -An index used to access an entry in a color table.

Color model -The method by which an application describes a color.

Color table -A workstation dependent table in which the entries specify the values defining a particular color.

Composite modeling transformation -A transformation applied to output primitives produced during structure traversal. It is defined as the concatenation of the local modeling transformation and global modeling transformations such that the local modeling transformation is the first transformation to be applied.

Conditional traversal -The process of selectively traversing structures or portions of structures based on some condition determined at traversal time. Specifically, in PHIGS+, condition flags can be used to control traversal.

Condition flags -An indexed set of boolean condition indicators that is part of the traversal state list. Some structure elements set or reset these indicators. Other structure elements refer to the condition flags to determine their effects.

Conflict resolution flag -During the process of structure archiving from the CSS or structure retrieval from an archive, naming conflicts may occur between structures on the archive file and structures in the CSS. The conflict resolution flag indicates how these conflicts will be resolved.

Connection identifier -An implementation specific means of defining the connection to one or more physical entities which constitutes a single workstation.

Cull -To replace the representation of one or more primitives by another typically simpler representation. PHIGS+ defines two types of culling: face culling and extent culling.

Cull size -An entry of the cull size table that is used as the threshold for extent culling.

D

Data record -A compound data type, the content of which is defined by the content within which it is used. For example, the content of the data records used in the input device initialization functions may vary depending on the particular prompt and echo type specified in the invocation of the initialization function.

Deferral mode -The deferral mode for a workstation is part of the display update state and specifies when changes to posted structure networks and the workstation state list will be reflected in the displayed image.

Depth cue -An effect in which the color of the primitives is combined with a specific depth cue color such that portions of primitives farther from the viewer are distinguishable from portions of primitives that are closer to the viewer. Depth cueing is applicable to all primitives in PHIGS+.

Depth cue mode -A field within a depth cue table entry that indicates whether depth cueing should be performed.

Depth cue planes -Two reference planes in NPC parallel to the X-Y plane at which depth cue scaling factors are specified.

Depth cue scaling factors -Weights that determine how the primitive's color is combined with the depth cue color to produce the depth cue effect. One scale factor is specified for each depth cue plane.

Depth cue table -A workstation dependent table, similar to the view table, which contains information necessary to control depth cueing.

Descendant structure -A child structure or the child of another child structure.

Device coordinates (DC) -A device dependent coordinate system. In PHIGS, DC units are metres on a device capable of producing a precisely scaled image and, otherwise, appropriate workstation dependent units otherwise.

Device driver -The device dependent part of a PHIGS implementation that supports a physical graphics device. The device driver generates device dependent output and handles device dependent interaction.

Device space -The space defined by the addressable points of a display device.

Diffuse reflection -An approximation of the light reflected equally in all directions from a surface. Diffusely reflected light gives a surface a dull matte appearance from all viewing angles.

Diffuse reflection coefficient -The fraction of light from non-ambient light sources diffusely reflecting from a surface.

Direct color -A nonindexed method of specifying color where the components of the color are specified together with the color model in which these components are expressed.

Display change mode -A part of the display update state. Display change mode specifies whether implicit regeneration will be POSTPONEd or ALLOWed.

Display device -A graphics device on which images can be represented. A display device is one possible component of a workstation.

Display priority -The priority assigned to a structure network when it is posted. It is used to discriminate between output primitives when they are mapped to the same display space location.

Display space -That portion of the device space corresponding to the volume available for displaying images.

Display surface -The physical area on a display device onto which PHIGS images may be placed.

Display update state -Determines how and when the display surface is modified to reflect changes in the centralized structure store and the workstation state list. An application selects the display update state to take into account the capabilities of a workstation and the requirements of the application program. The display update state consist of two workstation-dependent aspects of deferral mode and modification mode.

E

Echo -The immediate notification to the operator of the current measure of a logical input device.

Echo area; echo volume -An area or volume, defined in device coordinates, that may be used in the display of a prompt or echo.

Echo type -A parameter of device initialization that selects the echo technique for a particular logical input device.

Edge -The set of boundaries of the polygons defined in the fill area set primitive.

Edge flag -An aspect of the fill area set that enables or disables the display of edges.

Edgetype -An aspect of the fill area set that indicates the style of the edges.

Edgewidth scale factor -An aspect of the fill area set that indicates the relative width of the image of an edge. The edgewidth scale factor is applied to a workstation dependent nominal value.

Edit mode -Determines whether a new structure element will replace the structure element at the element pointer or will be inserted into the open structure after the element pointer.

Element pointer -A pointer used during structure editing, the value of that identifies the position in the open structure at which element deletion and creation will occur.

Element position -A number associated with a structure element that indicates the element's position within a structure.

Element reference list -A list of references which define the hierarchy within one branch of a structure network. Each reference consists of a structure identifier and an element position within that structure. If the path contains N pairs, then the first N-1 pairs identify EXECUTE STRUCTURE elements.

Element type -The identifying classification of a structure element. For example, fill area, label, application data, linewidth scale factor.

Empty interior style -One possible representation of the interior of a fill area or fill area set primitive. If the edges are not displayed, the image of a fill area set with interior style empty is invisible.

Error state list -The data holding information about the current error condition.

Escape -A function that provides access to implementation dependent or device dependent features, not concerned with the generation of graphical output.

Event mode -An operating mode for a logical input device in that asynchronous input is placed on the event queue as an event report when a trigger fires.

Event queue -A time-ordered collection of event reports.

Event report -An entry in the event queue that consist of a logical input value and identification of the logical input device responsible.

Exclusion set -The portion of a filter that defines those name set members that are not eligible for a certain operation.

Extent -A region within the coordinate space defined by a box whose edges are parallel to the coordinate axes. An extent is defined in PHIGS+ by the limits of the box in each dimension.

Extent culling -To replace or bypass traversal of a portion of a structure network when a particular volume would be displayed at less than a workstation-dependent size.

Eye point -The point used in the lighting calculation for determining view position dependent parts of lighting. This point is a point in WC that transforms to infinite positive Z in NPC.

F

Face culling -The process of making back-facing or front-facing primitives or portions of primitives invisible.

Fill area -An output primitive consisting of a single polygon.

Fill area set -An output primitive consisting of a set of fill areas.

Fill area set with data -An output primitive, consisting of a set of contours that is similar to fill area set primitive in PHIGS. The corresponding structure elements may include other information, such as color or normals, that may be used to light and shade the primitive.

Fill area with data -An output primitive, consisting of a single contour that is similar to fill area primitive in PHIGS. The corresponding structure elements may include other information such as color or normals that may be used to light and shade the primitive.

Filter -The combination of the inclusion set and the exclusion set that identifies primitives eligible or ineligible for a certain operation. PHIGS supports filters for picking, highlighting, visibility, and incremental spatial search.

Font -A set of character representations, all of which share certain visual characteristics.

Front face -Any portion of an area-defining primitive whose geometric normal when transformed to NPC has a nonnegative Z component. Front-facing portions of primitives can be made invisible.

Front plane -A plane parallel to the view plane, which is specified as an N coordinate value in the view reference coordinate system. Primitives in front of the front plane lie outside the view volume.

G

Generalized drawing primitive (GDP) -An output primitive that accesses implementation-dependent and workstation-dependent geometrical capabilities such as curve drawing.

Generalized structure element (GSE) -A structure element that is used to access implementation-dependent, workstation-dependent, or device-dependent features during structure traversal. It is a structure element that accesses attribute or control functionality, but does not create an output primitive.

Geometric normal -A vector that is, in principle, perpendicular to the plane containing a primitive, facet, or subprimitive. In PHIGS+, the geometric normal may be used in lighting calculations to determine whether vertex normals should be flipped, and to determine whether primitives or portions of primitives are back facing.

GKS -Graphics Kernel System.

Global modeling transformations -A component of the composite modeling transformation. When traversal of a structure begins, it is set to the current composite modeling transformation of the parent structure or if it is the posted structure, the default value in the PHIGS description table.

H

Hatch interior style -One possible representation of the interior of a fill area set or fill area primitive. The interior is filled with a pattern of parallel and/or crosshatch lines, selected from the workstation's hatch table.

Hatch table -The table of hatch values defined on a workstation.

Hidden-line/hidden-surface removal -Removal of those parts of output primitives that are obscured by other output primitives.

Highlighting -Emphasizing an output primitive by modifying its visual attributes in some workstation-dependent manner.

Highlighting filter -A filter consisting of two name sets, the highlighting inclusion set and the highlighting exclusion set, used to identify output primitives that are eligible for highlighting.

HLS -An abbreviation for the hue, lightness, and saturation color model.

Hollow interior style -One possible representation of the interior of a fill area or fill area set primitive. The image is the boundary line only, including any boundary lines included by clipping.

HSV -An abbreviation for the hue, saturation, and value color model.

I

Image -The appearance of an object after rendering.

Implicit regeneration -The complete recreation of the contents of the display surface such that it is visually correct. This may occur when changes to the posted structure networks or the workstation state list invalidate the displayed image. Such regeneration is not explicitly requested by the application program.

Inclusion set -The portion of a filter that defines those name set members eligible for a certain operation.

Infinite light source -A type of light source that enters into the lighting calculation dependent on the orientation of the surface being illuminated, but independent of the relative position of the surface being illuminated. This is used to simulate light sources relatively far from the surface being shaded.

Inheritance -The mechanism by which child structures obtain initial attribute settings from their ancestor structures.

Input class -The characterization of the functionality of a logical input device. There are six classes of logical input device: locator, stroke, valuator, choice, pick, and string.

Input mode -One of the three possible methods of obtaining data from a logical input device: REQUEST, SAMPLE, or EVENT.

Inquiry function -A mechanism for communicating to the application program data contained in a state list or description table.

Interior style -An aspect that indicates the style used to fill the interior of a fill area or a fill area set.

Invisibility filter -A filter consisting of two name sets, the invisibility inclusion set and the invisibility exclusion set, used to identify output primitives eligible for invisibility.

Isoparametric curve -The parametric curve that is produced from a parametric surface by holding one of the independent variables constant.

Isotropic mapping -A transformation that preserves aspect ratio.

L

Label -A structure element, consisting of an identifier, that can be used as a place-marker to facilitate structure editing.

Language binding -The expression of a functional specification in the syntax of a particular programming language.

Lighting -The effect of light sources on an area-defining primitive.

Lighting equation -A general formula through that the effect of lights illumination area-defining primitives is modeled.

Light source -An entry in a workstation light source table. Four types of light sources are defined: ambient, infinite, positional, and spot. All light sources have a color. Some light source types have a position, direction, concentration exponent, spread angle, and/or attenuation coefficients.

Line type -An aspect that indicates the style of the image of a polyline, such as solid, dashed or dotted.

Linewidth scale factor -An aspect that indicates the relative width of the image of a polyline. The linewidth scale factor is applied to a workstation dependent nominal value.

Local modeling transformation -A component of the composite modeling transformation. When traversal of a structure begins, it is set to the identity transformation.

Locator device -A logical input device providing a position in world coordinates and an associated view index.

Logical input device -An abstraction of one or more physical input devices that delivers logical input values to the application program.

M

Marker -A glyph with a specified appearance that is used to identify a location on the display surface. The shape of a marker is not subject to transformation.

Marker size scaler factor -An aspect that indicates the relative size of the image marker. The marker size scale factor is applied to a workstation dependent nominal value.

Marker type -An aspect that selects the type of glyph used.

Measure -A value that is determined by the values of one or more physical input devices and a mapping from these values to a form required by one of the logical input classes.

Measure process -A process that comes into existence when a logical input device is enabled for interaction. The current state of a measure process is the measure.

Message -A string sent by the application program to a workstation principally for communication with the operator.

Metafile -A mechanism for retaining and transporting graphical data and control information. This information contains a device independent description of one or more pictures.

Minimal solution -The minimal required action when the workstation does not have the capability to render an output primitive as specified by the application.

Modal -A type of change mechanism that extends its effect until another change specification supersedes it. Attribute settings and control functions are modal for a given structure and its descendant structures.

Modeling coordinates -The device-independent, three-dimensional Cartesian coordinate system in which graphical objects are defined by the application program using the PHIGS output primitives.

Modification mode -Part of the display update state. The modification mode governs which category of visual effects shall be immediately achieved and how it is achieved on a workstation.

N

Name set -A primitive attribute consisting of a set of classifications defining the eligibility of primitives for highlighting, invisibility, picking, and incremental spatial search.

Nominal value -The workstation-dependent base value for the following aspects of primitives: linewidth, marker size, and edgewidth.

Normal -A vector that is perpendicular to a surface at a specified location. In PHIGS+, the normal is used to specify the orientation of a surface for use in the lighting calculation. Using PHIGS+, an application can approximate a surface by fill area set with data primitives. In this case, the application could supply surface normals at each vertex to obtain a better visual representation. When this occurs, the normals are not necessarily perpendicular to the plane of the fill area set.

Normalized projection coordinates (NPC) -The device-independent three-dimensional Cartesian coordinate system in which the composition of images is specified to the graphical system. The view-clipping limits and the workstation window are specified in NPC space.

O

Output primitive -A fundamental graphical display entity representing a geometric shape.

P

Parallel transformation -The transformation of an object in which parallel lines in the object appear parallel in the resulting image without regard to relative distance or depth.

Parent structure -A structure that contains one or more structure references.

Pattern interior style -One possible representation of the interior fill area or fill area set primitive. The interior is filled in with a two-dimensional pixel pattern selected from the workstation's pattern table.

Pattern table -The table of pattern values defined for a workstation.

Perspective transformation -The transformation of an object in which parallel lines in the object that intersect the view plane appear to converge in the resulting image as a function of relative distance or depth.

Per vertex color -Direct color associated with each vertex of some area-defining primitives, such as polyline, fill area, fill area set, polyhedron, quadrilateral mesh, or triangle strip. The color is contained within the primitive definition and may be used as input to the rendering pipeline.

Per vertex normal -A 3-D vector that is associated with each vertex of some area-defining primitives, such as fill area with data, fill area set with data, polyhedron, quadrilateral mesh, or triangle strip. This vector will be used the surface normal or the primitive at the corresponding vertex. The vector is contained within the primitive definition and may be used in the lighting and shading stage of the rendering pipeline.

PHIGS -Programmers Hierarchical Interactive Graphics System.

PHIGS description table -The data that represents the static workstation independent parameters of a PHIGS system.

PHIGS traversal state list -The data that represent the dynamic workstation-independent parameters of a PHIGS system during traversal of a structure network. When traversal begins the PHIGS traversal state list values are set to the values defined in the PHIGS description table.

Physical input device -Hardware capable of generating input. A physical input device is either part of a display device or a separate part of the workstation.

Pick device -A logical input device providing a pick path.

Pick filter -A filter consisting of two name sets, the pick inclusion set and the pick exclusion set used to identify output primitives that are eligible for selection by a pick input operation.

Pick identifier -A name associated with individual output primitives and returned by a pick device as a component of the pick path.

Pick path -The traversal path to a picked output primitive from its posted structure, consisting of the structure identifier, pick identifier, and element position for each level of the hierarchy traversed.

Polyhedron -An output primitive in which a number of facets are defined by indexing into a single vertex list. Each facet is treated like a fill area set with data. The facets are not required to form a closed surface.

Polyline -An output primitive consisting of a connected sequence of straight lines between specified points.

Polyline set with data -An output primitive consisting of an unconnected set of polylines. The corresponding structure element may include other information, such as colors that may be used to shade the primitive.

Polymarker -An output primitive consisting of a set of locations, each indicated by the same type of marker.

Positional light -A type of light source that enters into the lighting calculation dependent on the orientation and relative position of the surface being illuminated.

Post -To identify a structure for display on a particular workstation.

Projection reference point (PRP) -A point in view reference coordinate space that determines the direction of projectors when the projection type is PARALLEL or from which all projectors emanate when the projection type is PERSPECTIVE.

Projection type -The type of transformation to be used in view mapping, that is, parallel transformation or perspective transformation.

Projection viewport -A rectangle parallelepiped in normalized projection coordinate space. In the PHIGS viewing model, the view mapping transformation maps the contents of the view volume into the projection viewport.

Projector -A conceptual line that passes through each point of an object and intersects the view plane.

Prompt -An operating mode for a logical input device in which PHIGS waits until the operator activates the appropriate trigger where upon the measure is returned.

Prune -To replace or bypass traversal of a position of a structure network when a particular extent is completely clipped by either the modeling clip planes, the view clipping limits, or the workstation transformation.

Pseudo coloring -The process of calculating a weighted average of the components of colors produced by the rendering pipeline to produce a single value that is used as an index into a table of colors whose content defines the actual color generated.

R

Rendering Color Model -The rendering color model in which any color interpolation by the rendering pipeline is performed. This includes the color interpolation which may be performed as part of the shading portion of the lighting and shading stage and the color interpolation that may be performed.

Rendering pipeline -A sequence of operations that performs lighting, shading, depth cueing, and color approximation of output primitives.

Request mode -An operating mode for a logical input device in which the measure of a logical input device may be obtained immediately without waiting for a trigger.

RGB -An abbreviation for the red, green, and blue color model.

S

Sample Mode -An operating mode for a logical input device in which the measure of a logical input device may be obtained without waiting for a trigger.

Shading -The interpolation porting of the rendering pipeline. Shading is applicable to area defining and polyline primitives.

Solid interior style -One possible representation of the interior style of a fill area or a fill area set primitive. The interior is filled with a uniform color.

Specular color -The color of specular highlights of a surface.

Specular exponent -A number representing the shine of a surface, such that the higher the specular exponent, the shinier the surface.

Specular reflection -An approximation of the light reflected from a surface that causes highlights on shinny objects. The intensity of specular reflections, unlike diffuse reflections, is highly dependent on the viewing angle of the observer.

Specular reflection coefficient -The fraction of light from nonambient sources specularly reflecting from a surface.

Spot light -A type of light source like a positional light source, but that also restricts the zone of illumination to a semiinfinite cone and/or concentrates the brightness of the light along a ray emanating from the light source position.

String device -A logical input device providing a string.

Stroke device -A logical input device providing a sequence of points in world coordinates, and an associated view index.

Structure -A linear sequence of structure elements.

Structure archiving -The process of storing structures and structure networks in an archive file for subsequent structure retrieval.

Structure editing -The modification of a structure, including its initial creation.

Structure element -The fundamental unit of data in the centralized structure store, a sequence of which is collected to form a structure. Structure elements include elements causing the generation of output primitives, attribute selections, labels, application data, NAME SET specifications, transformation selections, and structure references.

Structure identifier -A unique application specified name used to reference a structure.

Structure network -A collection of structures arranged with the topology of an acyclic directed graph, where structures are thought of as nodes and execute structure elements are thought of as connections from the parent structure to the child structure.

Structure reference -The invocation of one structure from within another by an execute structure element or the invocation of a structure by posting.

Structure state list -The data that represent information about each structure in the Centralized Structure Store.

Subprimitive -An implementation-dependent fragment that may be generated by the tessellation of a curve or surface primitive that is rendered in much the same way a polyline or fill area is rendered.

Surface properties -An attribute that defines the set of reflectance coefficients and other aspects that provide information about an area-defining primitive to the lighting and shading stage of the rendering pipeline. Surface properties include ambient reflection coefficient, diffuse reflection coefficient, specular reflection coefficient, specular color, specular exponent, and transparency coefficient.

T

Text -An output primitive consisting of a character string drawn at a specified position on a specified text plane.

Text alignment -An aspect of text that specifies the mode of justification. This aspect has horizontal and vertical components.

Text direction vectors -Two vectors, specified as part of the text structure element, which together with the text position define the text plane.

Text extent -A parallelogram defining the minimum area that completely encloses the character bodies in a string.

Text font -An aspect of text that indicates certain visual properties of a character, such as typeface.

Text path -An aspect of text that control the positioning of successive characters in a string.

Text plane -The plane in which a text primitive appears.

Text position -A point specified as part of the text structure element that together with the text direction vectors, determine the text plane. It also determines, together with text alignment, the location of the string.

Text precision -An aspect of text that selects the fidelity with which the drawing of a text primitive matches the appearance selected by an application program.

Transformation pipeline -The ordered sequence of transformations that convert's modeling coordinates to device converts.

Transparency -An approximation of the effect of transmitting light through a primitive.

Transparency coefficient -The fraction of light transmitted through a primitive.

Traversal -The process of stepping through a structure network, elaborating each structure element by generating an output primitive or changing state list.

Triangle strip -An output primitive in which n triangles are specified using n+2 points.

Trigger -A physical input device or set of devices that an operator can use to indicate significant moment in time.

Trigger process -A process that notifies an associated logical input device when a trigger is fired. The trigger process only exist when a device is in EVENT mode, or in REQUEST mode with a request pending.

Trimmed curve -A parametric curve defined in parameter space of the surface to which it applies. Trim curves are combined to form contours that limit the parameter range over which the corresponding surface is rendered.

Trimmed surface -A primitive that is defined by a parametric surface and a set of contours in parameter space. The contours specify the portions of parameter space over which the surface is rendered.

V

Valuator device -A logical input device providing a real number.

View index -A primitive attribute that selects the view representation applied to primitives and geometric attributes during structure traversal.

View mapping matrix -A 4X4 matrix that specifies the transformation of points from view reference coordinates to normalized projection coordinates.

View orientation matrix -A 4X4 matrix that specifies the conversion of points from world coordinates to view reference coordinates.

View plane -A plane parallel to the U-V plane in view reference coordinate space (VRC). It is specified as an N coordinate value in VRC.

View plane normal -A vector in world coordinates, relative to the view reference point, that defines the N coordinate axis in view reference coordinate space.

View reference coordinate (VRC) system -A device-independent three-dimensional Cartesian coordinates system in which the parameters for the view-mapping transformation are specified. The axes of the view reference coordinate system are called U,V, and N axes. The position and orientation of this coordinate system, relative to world coordinates, are defined by the view reference point, the view plane normal, and the view up vector.

View reference point -A point in world coordinates that defines the view reference coordinate system origin.

View representation -A single entry in the view table. It consist of the view orientation matrix, the view mapping matrix, the view-clipping limits, and a set of clipping indicators.

View table -The table of view representations defined on a workstation. Its entries are referenced by the view index attribute.

View transformation input priority -Determines the order in which view table entries are tested when selecting the inverse viewing transformation to be applied to locator and stroke input.

View-up vector -A vector defined in world coordinate space. The view reference coordinate system V coordinate axis is defined as an orthogonal projection of the view-up vector onto the plane through the view reference point and perpendicular to the view plane normal. Vectors that are parallel to the view up vector in world coordinate space will appear vertical in the final image.

View volume -The view volume is determined by the view window defined in the view plane, the front plane, the back plane and projectors all pass through the corners of the view window. If the projection type is PERSPECTIVE, the projectors all pass through the projection reference point, the view volume in this case is a parallelpiped. In two dimensional applications, the view volume reduces to the view window.

View window -A rectangle in the view plane. Projectors passing through the corners of the view window define the left, right, bottom, and top surfaces of the view volume.

Visually correct -The display on a workstation is visually correct when it corresponds exactly to the state of centralized structure store and the workstation state list.

W

Workstation -An abstract graphical resource that provides the logical interface through which the application program controls physical devices. A workstation consist of zero or one display space and zero or more logical input devices.

Workstation category -A property of a workstation that indicates whether it can perform graphics input only, graphics output only, or both.

Workstation description table -The data that represents capabilities for a particular workstation type.

Workstation identifier -A unique application specified name used to identify a particular workstation.

Workstation state list -The data that represents dynamic information for a particular workstation.

Workstation transformation -A transformation that maps the contents of the workstation window into the workstation viewport, preserving aspect ratio in X and Y, but not necessarily in Z.

Workstation type -A type or class of actual workstations, sharing common characteristics and single workstation description table.

Workstation viewport -A rectangular parallelpiped in device coordinate space. All graphics appear within this volume.

Workstation window -A rectangular parallelpiped in normalized projection coordinate space. Its contents are mapped by the workstation transformation into the workstation viewport.

World coordinates -The device independent three-dimensional Cartesian coordinates system used by the application program to organize modeled objects for display. The effect of applying the composite modeling transformation to modeling coordinates is to produce world coordinates.

Index